VOID
Library of
Davidson College

PREFECT AND EMPEROR

The *Relationes* of Symmachus
A.D. 384

A gold coin struck perhaps soon after A.D. 417 in honour of Galla Placidia, daughter of Theodosius I, wife of Constantius, later Constantius III, mother of Valentinian III. The emblems of the Cross and of the Winged Victory, one of the oldest themes of Roman coinage, are here shown together. Christianity was not yet able to supplant paganism in spite of imperial legislation; the solution was to combine them. The pagan goddess, with her wings, wreath, and palm, became, for Christians, an angel holding the Cross and symbolizing its victory. See especially *Relatio* 3 below

Photograph by courtesy of the Heberden Coin Room, Ashmolean Museum
Scale 2 : 1

PREFECT AND EMPEROR

The *Relationes* of Symmachus
A.D. 384

WITH TRANSLATION
INTRODUCTION AND NOTES BY
R. H. BARROW

OXFORD
AT THE CLARENDON PRESS
1973

Oxford University Press, Ely House, London W.1

GLASGOW NEW YORK TORONTO MELBOURNE WELLINGTON
CAPE TOWN IBADAN NAIROBI DAR ES SALAAM LUSAKA ADDIS ABABA
DELHI BOMBAY CALCUTTA MADRAS KARACHI LAHORE DACCA
KUALA LUMPUR SINGAPORE HONG KONG TOKYO

ISBN 0 19 814443 1

© *Oxford University Press 1973*

*All rights reserved. No part of this publication may be reproduced,
stored in a retrieval system, or transmitted, in any form or by any
means, electronic, mechanical, photocopying, recording or otherwise,
without the prior permission of Oxford University Press*

*Printed in Great Britain
at the University Press, Oxford
by Vivian Ridler
Printer to the University*

PREFACE

THE Latin text is that given in Otto Seeck's edition of Symmachus' works published by Messrs. Weidmann, of Berlin, in their series *Monumenta Germaniae historica*; it is reproduced without the full *apparatus criticus*.

Dr. J. F. Matthews, Fellow of Corpus Christi College, Oxford, advised the shortening of the introduction and notes to their present dimensions and gave generous help in many ways. I am very grateful to him.

The two books by A. Chastagnol cited on page 23 have been laid under contribution throughout; anyone using them cannot help being most indebted to their author.

R. H. B.

CONTENTS

FRONTISPIECE

A gold coin struck perhaps soon after A.D. 417 in honour of Galla Placidia, daughter of Theodosius I, wife of Constantius, later Constantius III, mother of Valentinian III

ABBREVIATIONS   xi

INTRODUCTION
The *Praefectura Urbana* in 384   1
Q. Aurelius Symmachus Eusebius   9
The *Relationes*   15
    The *Relationes* and their 'attached papers'   17
    The Text   19
    Editions   21
    Numeration   22
Select Bibliography   23
Table of Dates   25
Family Tree of the Emperors   26

THE *RELATIONES*
1. Thanks to Valentinian for the prefecture of the city   28
2. Thanks to Theodosius for the prefecture of the city   30
3. The Altar of Victory   32
4. The *carruca*   48
5. Commendation of Celsus the philosopher   52
6. Expectation of games   56
7. Thanks for an imperial New Year present   58
8. The senate and expenditure on games   60

CONTENTS

9. Praise for the imperial care for Rome in providing games, food, etc.   65
10. Announcement of the death of Praetextatus   72
11. Announcement of the death of Praetextatus   76
12. Asks that a statue may be put up to Praetextatus   78
13. The senate's contribution of gold to the *decennalia*   82
14. The requisitioning of horses is too much of a burden   86
15. *Strenae*   90
16. The appeal of Priscianus and Polemonianus   93
17. Better officials are needed   96
18. Anxiety about the corn-supply   98
19. The case of Marciana senior and junior   101
20. The problem of the silver for the *carruca*   109
21. Complaint about intrigues against Symmachus   113
22. The *tribunus fori suarii* and his removal from office; contradictory enactments   120
23. The humiliation of Symmachus by imperial officials in the matter of Memorius   122
24. Covering letter with a collection of speeches by Praetextatus   136
25. Inquiry into the collapse of a bridge   139
26. Inquiry into the collapse of a bridge   142
27. The seniority of a state doctor; contradictory enactments   148
28. A tangled case of *possessio*: Scirtius *v.* Olybrius and others   153
29. The rate of exchange needs revision   162
30. The persecution of two women of high rank by officials   164
31. The case of Valerianus, who consistently defied the laws   168
32. Appeal on a matter of renewal of time in a law-suit   170
33. The appeal of Constantius, *suarius*   174
34. The attack on the integrity of Orfitus is an attack on Symmachus   178

CONTENTS

35. Anxiety about the oil supply	190
36. Apology for delay	192
37. Dilatory payment of revenues from the provinces causes scarcity at Rome	194
38. The case of a decurion pretending to be a civil servant is beyond Symmachus' jurisdiction	196
39. A clash of constitutions in a matter of renewal of time	200
40. The dispute between Puteoli and Tarracina	205
41. The case of Aggarea	210
42. Commends a *cornicularius*	216
43. Reports equestrian statues of Valentinian I	218
44. The sharing of 'services' by two guilds	221
45. Covering letter to a return of recent appointments	224
46. Covering letter to a return of recent appointments	226
47. Congratulations on successful campaigns: the defeat of the Sarmatae	228
48. Complaint that the fisc tries to take cases involving senators to courts outside Rome	230
49. The case of a civil servant who made an ill-advised appeal	234
ADDITIONAL NOTES	238
GLOSSARY	240
SELECT INDEX	244

ABBREVIATIONS

Amm.	Ammianus Marcellinus
CIL	*Corpus Inscriptionum Latinarum*
CIust.	*Codex Iustinianus*
CTh.	*Codex Theodosianus*
Dess.	H. Dessau, *Inscriptiones Latinae Selectae*
Dig.	The *Digest* of Justinian
LSJ	Liddell–Scott–Jones, *A Greek–English Lexicon*
PLRE	Jones–Martindale–Morris, *The Prosopography of the Later Roman Empire*

Bold figures, e.g. **23**, refer to *Relationes*

INTRODUCTION

THE *PRAEFECTURA URBANA* IN 384

ANCIENT writers may have traced the beginnings of the prefecture back to Romulus (Tac. *Ann.* 6. 11), but as a permanent institution it dates from A.D. 13. Its history during the second, third, and early fourth centuries is complicated and in some respects obscure; the office was affected profoundly by the general changes in the machinery of government and administration. Reforms of 321, 326, and 357 established the main features of the office as it was held by Symmachus in 384.

At that time the office carried tremendous power and prestige: it was the summit of the senatorial career. Its holder was the Emperor's representative invested with the Emperor's delegated power and answerable only to him. The title was *praefectus urbi sacra vice iudicans* and, since the proconsulship of Africa was generally held before the prefecture, *iterum* was inserted before *iudicans*. The sphere was Rome and, for specified purposes, an area a hundred miles round Rome, and, as regards certain appeals, beyond that range. The prefect was the 'guardian of the city', its welfare was his care (Sen. *Ep.* 83. 14); his duty was to ensure the smooth running of its total life and his responsibility extended to every department of activity and to the details of each. His chief function was to administer justice and to see that the law was kept: but his supervision extended over the deliberations of the senate, the administration of government departments, the maintenance of the food supply, the efficient working of the guilds, games, public works, religious cult; personnel and finance were under his general control. It was his duty to report regularly to the Emperor the proceedings of the senate, appointments to it and to the magistracies (**45, 46**), and to convey to him the feelings of the populace as expressed by *acclamationes* in the Circus (**9. 8,**

10. 2) and elsewhere: similarly he was the channel through which the Emperor conveyed his wishes to senate and people.

In practice, however, the office was severely limited. Its holder was appointed by the Emperor and remained during his pleasure. His authority was delegated and it was not easy to know when it was being exceeded; Ammianus says of Orfitus that 'he behaved with an arrogance which went beyond the limits of his delegated position' (14. 6. 1). The prefect had to take the law as it stood, and conflicting rescripts made interpretation difficult, e.g. **22, 27.** 4, **30.** 4: he could not make law, he could only apply it. He pronounced judgement and prescribed penalties only when guilt was patent, and his judgements were subject to appeal. His actions were open to constant surveillance. The permanent officials of the departments, whom he did not appoint, could criticize him, make decisions without reference to him (**23.** 2, **37.** 2), place obstacles in his way, and report to the Emperor. If he complained of their incompetence (**17**) or ill-will, he was liable to reprimand.

Besides these officials, established, opposed to change, and jealous of vested interests, there were others who owed immediate allegiance to superiors in a chain which led up to the praetorian prefect or the *magister officiorum*. Their duties and powers were sometimes parallel to those of the prefect and his staff and sometimes they overlapped. These officials often acted as spies and informers. The most powerful was the *vicarius* who was supposed to act as assistant to the prefect, but, as he had his own tribunal and staff, it was easy for him to be a rival or opponent. Others were the *agentes in rebus, tribuni et notarii* (**23**) who could conduct their own inquiries, besides officials of the fisc and palatine servants of lower degree. Sometimes a *comes* was sent on a special mission to investigate a prefect's conduct (**23.** 1). Nor could a prefect always rely on the loyalty of those whom in particular he felt himself to represent (**48.** 1): twice Symmachus complains of the defiance of senators (**23, 31**), while Celsus, a barrister in the prefect's court, was the friend of the *vicarius* and was

given promotion by the Emperor in spite of Symmachus' adverse report on him (23).

Finally, the climate of opinion hampered or helped a prefect. Much depended on the attitude of the Emperor: he might be anti-senatorial and anti-pagan, or the reverse, and his attitude was reflected in his behaviour to his prefect. He could stimulate the independent activities of his agents who would be quick to take their cue. Indeed, Symmachus complains that the Emperor had reprimanded him in a rescript which he had to communicate publicly to senate and people (**21.** 2); on another occasion one of his functions was temporarily handed over to the *vicarius* (**33.** 2). These were times when feeling rapidly changed. In the summer of 384 the pagan party felt themselves strong enough to warrant the dispatch of 3, but three months later a change had set in, and the *Relationes* of the second part of Symmachus' tenure of office reflect despondency and frustration. The climate at court had altered, thanks largely to the efforts of Ambrose, and quarters inimical to Symmachus and his friends gained courage in resisting him.

If then the *Relationes* seem cautious and perhaps timid, the limitations on the powers of the prefect and the opportunities for misrepresentation of him by imperial agents must be taken into account; see especially **21, 23**. He was compelled to walk warily. Moreover, the dispatches record only the legal cases which Symmachus referred; how many he dealt with himself we cannot estimate.

Justice. The main functions of the prefect were judicial. Within his area—Rome and a hundred miles round about— he was supreme judge. Naturally much was delegated to local judges, to the *praefectus annonae* or *praefectus vigilum* or *vicarius* or *praetor*; but he could call for any case to be referred to him, and the most important he reserved for himself. In cases of embezzlement or treason (**36**) the prefect shared in the investigation, but the Emperor decided and sentenced. Murder, poisoning, kidnapping (*plagium*), *invasio* or the

INTRODUCTION

attempt to turn someone out of possession (i.e. occupation) of property (**38, 49**), the disputes of bankers or money-changers (**29**) were sent to him. Questions of liberty and manumission were normally handled by the praetors but went to the prefect on appeal: praetors nominated *curatores* and *procuratores* for women and could decide whether a mandate was valid (**19.** 2, 3). Complaints about 'undutiful wills' and 'excessive gifts' went to the prefect (**16, 19.** 7); in matters relating to ownership he could also pronounce (**16, 19**).

From 361 the scope for appeal from other courts within the hundred miles was much widened. The prefect could hear even fiscal cases (**41**), and could receive appeals from the *vicarius* (**38, 40**). But between the two judges there could be rivalry, though sometimes they sat together on the same bench, and once at least a matter within the competence of the prefect was handed over by the Emperor to the *vicarius* (**33.** 2). And the *comes rei privatae* showed resentment that appeals concerning its interest should go to the prefect (**33**).

Clarissimi were tried by the prefect within his area; in civil cases a *clarissimus* in the proconsular provinces was assumed to have his *domicilium* in Rome, and so the prefect could claim the right to try him on the principle that the prosecution must go to the court in the defendant's place of residence (**31, 48.** 2).

Police. The *cohortes urbanae* and the *vigiles* had been reshaped before 384: the *cohortes* were absorbed into the *officium urbanum* (**42**), their members becoming civil servants in uniform and being known as *contubernales*. The duties of the *vigiles*, who operated only at night, were taken over by selected members of the *corpora* or guilds. The *contubernales* were commanded by the *tribunus fori suarii*, and the *corporati* by the *praefectus vigilum* who retained his old title; both officers were subordinate to the prefect.

Religion. Since the consuls now spent their time with the Emperor away from Rome and other magistracies had become less important, religious ceremonies, which were

4

necessarily connected with the state, tended to be taken over by the prefect. He continued to preside at festivals: the priesthoods continued to function, but temples and all that went on in them and in the sacred colleges were in the last resort the prefect's responsibility. As Christianity grew to an equality with paganism, the link between paganism and the state became all the clearer and the prefect's position became more difficult. Valentinian I may have been praised by Ammianus (30. 9) for his neutrality, but by implication he had given official recognition to Easter (*CTh.* 9. 38. 3, 4) and he established *defensores ecclesiae*. The prefect was compelled to take part in the struggle between Damasus and Ursinus for the bishopric of Rome. But it was Gratian who broke the association of state and paganism: he refused to be Pontifex Maximus, confiscated the revenues and immunities of temples and priesthoods, and rejected protest (**3**). Henceforth all acts of a pagan nature were to be separated from the state: the prefect could preside at the games but offer no sacrifice: temples became imperial property and had to be privately maintained, if at all. The *curator operum publicorum*, who acted under the prefect, could now concern himself only with Christian churches, not with temples. Symmachus and his predecessors were concerned with the building of a *basilica* ordered by Valentinian II (**25. 2**). For a moment Praetextatus won the concession that statues and material plundered from temples should be restored (**21. 5**); pagan hopes of resistance were high in the summer of 384 but soon fell as the power of Ambrose increased and Symmachus was succeeded by a Christian *praefectus urbi*, Pinianus. This meant to Symmachus that the state and the old gods would no longer be associated, that, if the gods were not the state's gods, worship of them would no longer be effective of the state's good, that the state without the gods could not prosper.

The sustenance of Rome. The tranquillity of the city was assured only if the populace was fed, provided with necessities, and amused—holidays took up nearly half the year. The

prefect was always in a state of nervousness, for he perpetually feared upheaval and rioting for one reason or another (**6, 9, 18, 35**). Gratian made the prefect ultimately responsible for the smooth working of the system and for its finance; details of administration he entrusted to the *praefectus annonae* of the area. At the same time he cut off supplies from Egypt, Spain, and Campania (**37. 2, 40.** 4), and made Rome dependent on Africa only. In time of famine the Emperor made gifts from elsewhere, and famine was frequent; Symmachus himself had to ask for special help (**6. 2, 18. 37**). In Africa control lay with the proconsul and the *praefectus annonae* there, who was subordinate to the *praefectus praetorio* of Italy–Africa. The corn was brought to Ostia and Portus by *navicularii*, some of whom were *clarissimi* and may themselves have owned corn-producing estates. The prefect gave notice of the requirements of Rome and neighbouring cities (**35. 2**). Before 356 the prefect and the *praefectus annonae*—Cerealis in 328—fixed the contribution of Campania, and after Julian the praetor was concerned (**40.** 3). At Ostia the ships were welcomed by the prefect or his representative (**9**). The corn was handled by *saccarii* (= *baiuli*) whose interests Symmachus protected (**3.** 15, **14.** 3). The *arca frumentaria*, office and granary, controlled the bakers (*pistores*), who drew flour from the stores, and probably other guilds, as for example *mensores*: the guilds were carefully watched by the prefect and officials of the *arca*, for evasion was not uncommon (**23.** 3).

In times of scarcity the prefect intervened: he could buy corn elsewhere, if possible: he could make a levy on senators or expel all foreigners (as indeed Symmachus did) or ask the Emperor for aid. In 384 the *arca frumentaria* was exhausted, partly because Gratian had cut off supplies from Egypt and Spain, partly because of the conduct of Bassus or, as it turned out, of his officials in 382 (for this matter see on **23**).

Oil was brought from Spain and Africa (**35**) and distributed in much the same way as the corn: there were daily distributions, for which some payment was probably made.

INTRODUCTION

The *arca vinaria* was an important fund; it was responsible for the supply of wine and meat, chiefly pork, and also for public buildings (see below). It controlled the guilds connected with these services, as, for example, *tabernarii, suarii*. Wine was brought by the growers from designated districts to Rome: if they could not furnish wine, they could pay a cash equivalent fixed by the Emperor. It was sold by *tabernarii* at a rate one-quarter below the market-rate; the amount of small change so collected, was exchanged for the *solidi* which came into the hands of money-changers; see **29**.

Public Buildings, Aqueducts, etc. The prefect had not enough funds to pay for new buildings: he had to borrow from the senatorial treasury (*arca quaestoria*) or from the aqueduct fund or from bankers, but more particularly from the *arca vinaria*. It was a continuing deficit in this account, incurred for public works, which gave rise to the 'Orfitus affair' (**34**): the difficulties which arose in building a bridge are seen in **25, 26**. The aqueducts (*formae*), under a *consularis aquarum*, supplied Rome and the neighbourhood with the quantity of water determined by the prefect: *mancipes thermarum* looked after the baths, while *mancipes salinarum* (**14. 3**) had the right to sell salt in special shops as a state-monopoly. The wood for heating the baths came from Africa, with a little from Campania (**40. 3**). The guilds operating these services were under the prefect's control (**44**). He was also responsible for the safety of river-banks in time of flood; private houses came under his supervision.

Games. Games were almost as important as food and gave the prefect similar cause for anxiety. Apart from those provided by the fisc, newly appointed magistrates had to incur great expense for this purpose. Praetors, for example, had to attend their games in person or be liable to a large fine. They could arrange for games to be organized on their behalf by the *censuales* (**8. 3, 23. 2**). This was a department which among other duties kept records of senators' property and incomes. Symmachus' anxiety is shown by **6**, in which

INTRODUCTION

he begs the Emperor to send a supply of wild beasts for the arena (cf. 7 and 9). During the days of excitement and amid the rivalries of the *factiones* order had to be maintained. The prefect's responsibility extended to the smallest details, even to ensuring that the names of race-horses were not changed.

The prefect's oversight extended in many other directions —medical services (27), teachers and students (5), libraries, weights and measures, and so on. With a loyal and disciplined staff carrying out a closely co-ordinated system of administration a prefect might have been able to carry out his task with some effectiveness. As it was circumstances were against him; Rome lived under a suffocating network of regulations which he could not enforce or abolish.

Officium urbanum. The prefect relied on his staff working in various centres. He would have liked to exert greater control over them (34. 6); they did in fact come under his jurisdiction as regards crime, but that did not ensure the smooth day-to-day work of an office. Their chief centre was at the *secretarium Tellurense*, or the *urbana sedes*, not far from the Baths of Trajan. Here the prefect and the *vicarius* shared a judicial bench and here were the *scrinia*—sub-departments; there was another 'communal bench' at the Circus Maximus (23. 9) and no doubt elsewhere. The *censuales* had their office close to the *Curia*, the *contubernales* in the *castra urbana* in the *Campus Martius*; other officials were scattered over the area as their duties required—accountants, book-keepers, and clerks of various grades concerned with the distribution of food and wine and the administration of every aspect of life. At the head of the main office was the *princeps*, an *agens in rebus* appointed by the Emperor: below him were the regular civil servants in a hierarchy—*cornicularius*, *commentariensis*, *numerarius*, the chief of whom was called *primiscrinius*, a title also given to the chief *adiutor* (23. 6, 7; 34. 6); then came very many other grades—*exceptores* (stenographers), *nomenclatores* (23. 8), and many more who made up the total staff (*apparitores*). The *princeps* could arrest a person (23. 11, 12),

INTRODUCTION

but his duties were chiefly official. He was a *perfectissimus* and on retirement could become *consularis* and *clarissimus*.

The *cornicularius* was the senior man of the permanent office staff. He too was *perfectissimus* and on retirement might become an *agens in rebus*; perhaps this appointment is meant in **42**. The *adiutor primiscrinius* was concerned with questions of banishment and with the citation of witnesses (**23.** 6, 7). The *numerarius* was responsible enough to have had charge of the *arca vinaria* (**34.** 6) and would have been expected to make good any deficit, together with the prefect.

These officials were paid in money and in kind: their service was *militia* and they wore the military *cingulum* instead of the *pallium*.

The prefect was attended by lictors and rode officially in a *carpentum* until Gratian ordered that a *carruca* should be equipped for him; in spite of Symmachus' protest (**4**) the *carruca* became the normal conveyance for the prefect.

Q. AURELIUS SYMMACHUS EUSEBIUS

Symmachus was born about 340,[1] the son of L. Aurelius Avianius Symmachus Phosphorius, *praefectus urbi* 364-5,[2] and his mother was (probably) a daughter of Fabius Titianus, prefect in 340. His grandfather was Aurelius Celsinus, prefect 341-2 and 351, and his great-grandfather M. Aurelius Nerius Symmachus, *vicarius* of Macedonia in 318-19 and a senator. The family can perhaps be traced back to Severan times when it was already senatorial.

He had two brothers who died before 380 and a third, Celsinus Titianus, who died as *vicarius* of Africa in 380. He married, either in 370 or 375, Rusticiana, the daughter of Memmius Vitrasius Orfitus, prefect 353-6 (**34.** 8, 10, and

[1] Apart from the necessarily factual account presented now in *PLRE*, pp. 863 ff., the best life of Symmachus is still that given (in Latin) in Seeck's introduction to his edition, supplemented or amended by his own *Regesten* and by A. Chastagnol, *Les Fastes*, with one or two additions by MacGeachy, see p. 23. Stemmata are given in Seeck, Chastagnol, op. cit., and *PLRE*, but they differ in many respects.

[2] Dess. 726, 769, 1257. For Symmachus' career see Dess. 2946.

note). There were two children; the elder was a daughter, name unknown, who married in 392-4 (or perhaps 388) Nicomachus Flavianus iunior; this marriage was commemorated by the diptych *Symmachi-Nicomachi* preserved in the Cluny and the Victoria and Albert Museums.[1] The younger was Q. Fabius Memmius Symmachus, born in 383, quaestor in 393 and praetor in 401.

Of the early life of Symmachus nothing is known. He held the quaestorship and in 365 was appointed *corrector* of Lucania and Brittium. In 369 he was chosen by the senate to present the *aurum oblaticium* to Valentinian I at Trèves to mark his *decennalia*; he must have acquired already some fame as an orator, for he was required to compose the panegyrics on Valentinian and Gratian of which fragments remain (*Or.* i and iii). He seems to have stayed at court for a little time where he became friendly with Ausonius; both were sent on a campaign[2] against the Alamanni. At this time he was made *comes tertii ordinis*, not a very high distinction for him, for it gave entry to the senatorial order and Symmachus was already a senator. He delivered a third panegyric in honour of Valentinian (*Or.* ii) probably on 1 January 370 and returned to Rome. He may then have married Rusticiana.

In 373 he became proconsul of Africa (his tenure is attested for 30 November, *CTh.* 12. 1. 73) and was succeeded, by 7 September 374, by the Christian Constantius, though he stayed in the province till the spring of 375. He seems to have stood well with Theodosius,[3] the father of the Emperor, who at the time was engaged in suppressing the rising of the pretender, Firmus (Sym. *Ep.* 10. 1. 2). The assembly of the province proposed to put up a statue of him when he

---

[1] For this diptych see M. H. Longhurst, *Catalogue of the Ivory Carvings in the Victoria and Albert Museum* (London, i, 1927): W. F. Volbach, *Elfenbeinarbeiten der Spätantiken und des frühen Mittelalters* (Mainz, 1952).

[2] But the campaign may have been only a conducted tour of inspection, see J. F. Matthews, *Western Aristocracies and the Imperial Courts, 365-425* (forthcoming).

[3] See J. F. Matthews, *Historia*, xix (1970), 464 ff.

relinquished office, but the proposal was vetoed by one of his rivals, perhaps Constantius (*Ep.* 9. 115).

Between 373 and 384 Symmachus held no office. His father had incurred the displeasure of the mob by an ill-judged remark at a time of shortage of wine in 375; his house was burnt and he was driven from Rome. Later it repented, called for the punishment of the rumour-mongers, and the senate voted his recall and recommended him for the consulship (Amm. 27. 3. 3; Sym. *Ep.* 1. 44. 1, 2. 38). Symmachus read to the senate the *oratio* sent by Gratian after the death of Valentinian in which he announced his future policy, and delivered to the people a speech in which he supported the application of Trygetius for the praetorship; its main point, however, was to thank the senate for recalling his father. Later in 376 he delivered *Oratio* iv in which he thanked the Emperor and the senate for nominating his father as consul for the following year. His father died towards the end of the year before assuming office. In 379 Symmachus read to the senate the Emperor's report of the victories of Gratian over the Alamanni and of the newly elevated Theodosius over the Goths.

In 382 he was sent by the senate to plead with Gratian for the re-erection of the Altar of Victory in the senate house, but largely owing to the influence of Ambrose he was refused audience (**3. 1, 20**).

His tenure of the prefecture of the city is to be dated from the end of June or the beginning of July 384 to January or February 385. This period of seven months or so falls into two roughly equal parts; in the first the hopes of the pagan party were high, and for this reason the plea for the restoration of the altar and the return of revenue to priesthoods was made to the new Emperor. In the second part the Christian party at court had increased its influence; direct attack and underhand intrigue against the prefect and his administration and the pagan cause which he supported became more common.[1] The change of climate is reflected in the *Relationes*,

[1] See H. Bloch in 'The pagan revival . . .' cited on p. 23.

as will be seen. A few months before Symmachus was appointed prefect, his great friend Praetextatus had become *praefectus praetorio* of Italy, Africa, and Illyria, and had obtained from Valentinian an order for the restoration of ornaments stolen from the temples (21). Here was another reason for the confidence of the pagan party. But Praetextatus died in December 384, and his death was a great grief to Symmachus, and seems to have been a deciding factor when he asked to be relieved of his post (10, 21). To this cause must be added the discomfort of his position; he felt himself subjected to the growing attacks of his enemies and to the declared opposition of the officials with whom he had to work (21, 23, 34).

Relieved of his office, to which Pinianus, a Christian, succeeded, Symmachus withdrew to his estates in Campania. At the beginning of 387 he went to Milan to attend the celebration of Valentinian's third consulship; when the pretender Maximus descended upon Italy, Symmachus supported him, even going so far as to pronounce a panegyric of him, probably at Milan. This he had reason to regret; for Maximus was defeated by Theodosius, and Symmachus took refuge in a Christian church. Thanks to the intervention of a Novatian bishop, Leontius, he was pardoned and showed his gratitude by writing a panegyric of Theodosius. He was nominated for the consulship for 391, and took the opportunity to ask once again for the restoration of the altar, for at the moment Theodosius and Ambrose were at variance. Again he was unsuccessful, for the Emperor and bishop soon became reconciled; he became consul in 391.

In 393 he again supported a pretender Eugenius, though with greater discretion than before: his son-in-law, Nicomachus Flavianus, who was prefect of Rome at the time, signified his support more openly and was punished by Theodosius after the defeat of Eugenius. Symmachus now spent his time on his Italian estates or in Rome: in 395, when famine was causing riots in Rome, the senate sent for him; he calmed their fears and organized collections of food.

INTRODUCTION

A year or two later, when Gildo overran north Africa and cut off Rome's corn supply, Symmachus persuaded the senate to declare Gildo a public enemy and so to declare its loyalty to the reigning Emperors. To meet the threat Stilicho required men for his army and he demanded them from the estates of senators. Symmachus managed to arrange that money should be accepted rather than men. But senate and people blamed him for their hardships since he had persuaded them to oppose Gildo. The people drove him from the city but later relented.

From 398 he was busy making preparations for the games to be given by his son as praetor in 400, but postponed till 401. He was present in Milan at the celebrations for Stilicho's consulship and early in 402 he again went to the capital as the senate's envoy to ask for the restoration of the Altar of Victory. He returned a sick man and, as nothing further is heard of him, presumably he died then.

Symmachus and his society

Symmachus belonged to a society ennobled by public office, and to an inner circle of that society held together by intermarriage and a shared refusal to abandon the institutions, traditions, literature, and outlook of the past. Backward-looking, defensive, proud, they believed that Rome had grown great under divine guidance. Like Praetextatus, some of them were ready to adopt oriental cults and to undergo the rites prescribed by them: they resisted Christianity not as such, but because it strove to usurp the place of the ancient Roman cults as the religion of the state; the gods would deny their aid unless recognized by the state as its authors and sustainers. Many of them were devoted to Latin literature and Roman history: the pages of Macrobius' *Saturnalia* show them immersed in matters of language and literature and religion and history, though mainly in Vergil; they set in hand the recension of the texts of Latin writers.[1]

---

[1] For a brief account see L. D. Reynolds and N. G. Wilson, *Scribes and Scholars*, pp. 32-5.

INTRODUCTION

In social life they maintained the manners of the past. They were rich and expected the power which riches had given them to continue to be theirs; Symmachus himself, though he possessed three houses in Rome and twenty-eight in Italy, was by no means the richest.[1] Significant events often escape the notice of contemporaries, but it is odd that in the letters of Symmachus the invasions of Goths and Franks, a change of Emperor, Christianity, decisive battles are not mentioned.[2] In modern times there are social gatherings at which people of different views meet—to celebrate an anniversary, the launching or the completion of a project, or the success of an individual; in deference to the harmony and fellowship of the occasion no reference would be made, even in conversation, to matters which might none the less be in the minds of all; good taste would forbid it. Turn this temporary attitude of mind into a permanent habit of life shared by numerous families conscious of rank and office, and it is possible to feel something of the spirit pervading a society which was anxious to preserve standards in a turbulent world. Good feeling may have become frozen into formality, restraint into immobility, yet certain values remained. No society which is being elbowed out has the courage to contemplate its own disappearance; it still believes that something can be preserved. Symmachus and his friends pursued their way unruffled, at least to outward appearance, and to them appearance was a part of the struggle. There was a reticence, an inarticulate feeling, at any rate among the older and prouder families, that Emperors came and went, wars or famines occurred or did not, but Rome and the senate and a way of life were permanent and important above all else. We may say that Symmachus and his friends made a brave attempt, or we may say, in the light of events, that they were blind.

[1] Olympiodorus, fr. 44.
[2] After referring briefly to the disaster at Hadrianopolis in 378 Symmachus continues 'nos ad familiaria revertamur', *Ep.* 3. 47.

INTRODUCTION

THE *RELATIONES*

The forty-nine *Relationes* were the official dispatches sent by Symmachus to the Emperor. A third of them are on legal matters, two are covering letters sent with official returns, a few send greetings, thanks, or presents offered in the name of the senate: many were accompanied by summaries of evidence and statements which we do not possess.

Apparently Symmachus intended to publish his letters, and he divided the private letters into nine books and reserved the official dispatches for the tenth book: in this arrangement he was imitating Pliny. But he left them in an untidy state: some of the dispatches are addressed to Emperors to whom they could not have been sent, most have no addressee, and they are not in chronological order. Moreover, sometimes the title does not always agree with the abbreviated form 'd. n.' or 'dd. nn.' in the body of the dispatch. Publication of letters and dispatches was undertaken by his son[1] who seems to have left the letters as he found them, except that he probably gathered together those addressed to the same person and almost certainly cut out passages which might be politically embarrassing to him or to the memory of his father, notably in regard to Eugenius. There are about nine hundred private letters.

All the *Relationes*, with the exception of 9 and 42, were written for the attention of Valentinian II. They may have been addressed to more than one Emperor, but this practice was in deference to the principle of the 'collegiality' of the Emperors. In fact, their subject-matter could be of concern only to the Emperor of the West and to his officials, and behind the formal language a direct approach to an individual can often be detected. Moreover, the somewhat prevalent estimate of the dispatches as timid and hesitating needs correction. It is true that in legal matters Symmachus did ask for a ruling; but that was because contrary enactments had placed a matter beyond the scope of legal

[1] Stated in manuscript P at the beginning of the 3rd, 5th, and 10th books.

INTRODUCTION

argument and all that remained was the cutting of the knot by the supreme legislative authority. He is quite ruthless in pointing to the inconsistencies of imperial legislation. Elsewhere he shows tact and courage. He makes his own view clear and he quietly indicates the opening which the Emperor might see fit to take. He does not hesitate to attack important people who might stand well in court circles or to criticize the Emperor's own appointments and the behaviour of his officials. He shows the necessary politeness, but he retains for himself a high degree of independence which does not hesitate to take the initiative.

If it be taken into account that the political and religious climate changed to the prejudice of the pagan cause about half-way through Symmachus' tenure of office, a rough chronological order can be established for about twenty of the dispatches: some carry internal evidence of date.

1, 2	early: thanks for appointment.
4	early: Symmachus would protest about the *carruca* as soon as possible.
25	if on the flight of Auxentius *sub ipso aestatis exordio* Symmachus wrote at once, the dispatch would be dated in June.
8	if Symmachus' proposals inspired *CTh.* 15. 9. 1 and 6. 4. 25, this dispatch would be dated before 25 July.
3	summer, just after the harvest.
18	a little after **3**, perhaps Sept., cf. *aestate provecta*.
35	soon after **18**: the dearth of oil would be felt after the corn-harvest. Yet the seas were open. Sept.?
16, 28	before 29 Nov. since a law of that date had not been passed.
13	a little before 22 Nov., the date of Valentinian's *decennalia*.
23	Oct. or Nov.? after **13**.
21	before the end of Nov. or Dec. since Praetextatus

INTRODUCTION

and Damasus are spoken of as alive, and Praetextatus died in Nov. or Dec., and Damasus in Dec. The circumstances are unfavourable to Symmachus and his party.

10, 11, 12, 24	after the death of Praetextatus.
34	about the same time as 10.
17, 22	Oct. or Nov.?
23	before 1 Feb. 385 since it must be before a law of that date.
7, 15	*strenae* would be sent before 1 Jan. 385.
33	after 29 Nov. See 16.
45	after 9 Jan. 385 since senators were appointed on that day.

The Relationes *and their 'attached papers'*

There is nothing in the *Relationes* themselves to show whether they were written on rolls or in codices except the references to the documents which Symmachus says he attaches to some of them. For *pagina* does not imply the form of the codex; *pagina* was not a 'leaf' of a book but was a block or column of writing, and therefore could be used of a roll or a codex.

In his fascinating study of 'The Codex' (*Proc. of British Academy*, xl. 169–204) C. H. Roberts sums up as follows: 'The roll still survived in the fourth century although it was rapidly losing ground. As time went on it was increasingly restricted to formal, diplomatic, and liturgical purposes' (p. 203). The *Relationes* were formal and diplomatic; if it is assumed that they were written on rolls of papyrus, the assumption may be converted into proof by consideration of the terms which Symmachus used to denote 'attachment' of supplementary 'papers'. The terms are as follows:

19 Coniunctae paginae allegationes partium et supplementa sumpserunt; **24** subditis exemplaribus gestorum; **26** nonnulla indiciis intimavit quae ideo gestorum paginis placuit adplicari; **27** subditis allegationibus partium summam negotii reservavi; **28** gesta et supplementa partis utriusque subieci; **32** lectis gestis

ac refutatoriis cohaerentibus; **33** omnium gestorum fida documenta cum supplementis partium relationi ex more sociata sunt; **37** omnibus quae cohaerent libenter inspectis; **39** gestis omnibus de more subiectis; **41** relatione summatim cuncta complexus gestorum quoque documenta subtexui; **46** instructio quam ... paginis relationis adnexui; **45** his (sc. games and names of new appointments to office) copulati sunt quos (sc. new members of senate); **49** relationi gesta subtexui, partium quoque supplementa sociavi.

A note in *Corpus Glossariorum Latinorum* (ed. G. Goetz) iii. 153. 7; ii. 8. 47, says that *applico* and *adglutino* are the equivalent of προσκολλῶ, to glue one thing to another.[1] The adjective συγκολλησιμός is applied to τόμος (roll) and to βιβλιδία (P. Grenf. 2. 41. 18, 1st cent., P. Oxy. 2131. 4, 3rd cent., cited in LSJ) and means 'glued together'. *Adglutino* is not used by Symmachus, but occurs in Cic. *Att.* 16. 6 *ad fin.*, 'tu illud (prooemium) desecabis, hoc agglutinabis'. Cicero has sent Atticus a treatise complete with a *prooemium*; later he thinks a different *prooemium* would suit better, and so he asks him to cut off the original one and paste at the beginning of the roll another which he now sends him. Cicero's word is *adglutino*; Symmachus uses *applico* in the same sense. It is true that *applico* is also used in a more general sense as, for example, 'verba verbis applicare' in Quint. *Inst.* 7. 10. 17; but in *Inst.* 7. 3. 19 'est in hoc fere labor maior est ut finitionem confirmas quam ut in rem finitionem adplices': the idea is almost of a physical 'tacking on'. In Symmachus *coniungo* could be a less technical variant of *applico*, and *cohaereo* could be virtually a passive of *applico*.

We must assume, then, that the supplementary 'papers' were attached by gluing a sheet of papyrus to the end of the roll; to this extra sheet further sheets were successively attached.

Subdo, subicio, subtexo seem to be used in the general sense of 'add, subjoin, append' without any suggestion of a par-

[1] This reference and that to τόμος συγκολλησιμός are owed to C. H. Roberts; they are the most important references in this consideration of the terms.

INTRODUCTION

ticular physical method. *Subtexo* had long lost its original meaning (see examples cited in Lewis & Short). The Greek was ὑποτίθημι, cf. ὑποτέθεικά σοι τὸ ἀντίγραφον, P. Lille 4. 2 (3rd cent.) and other references in LSJ.

Many of the *Relationes* were concerned with complicated legal questions, and it is clear that Symmachus 'attached' reports of evidence to his own summary of the case. It is likely that some of the documents when assembled would exceed the capacity of a single roll of convenient size; or the documents might be in different rolls (made in different courts, for example) which it would be unnecessary to copy; all could be forwarded to the Emperor together. Perhaps this is the meaning of *socio*, to 'parcel' together, though how the parcel was made is a matter for conjecture. In a library rolls were kept in *capsae* or *scrinia* (*scrinia* probably held several rolls); to travel safely they must have been kept in some kind of container. Normally *capsae* were cylindrical cases (we do not know what they were made of); perhaps *socio* means to tie up two or more rolls with a string; the string might be sealed and the whole conveyed as one 'parcel'. Or there may have been a larger *capsa* to contain more than one roll.

The amount of 'book-work' done in government offices, in the army and ordinance depots, in municipal departments, in factories and trading-houses must have been enormous; of important documents copies had to be kept, as was true of the *Relationes* themselves. It is surprising that the supplies of papyrus and vellum were sufficient.[1] Materials could indeed be cleaned, or over-written, but there was a limit to such economy.

The Text

Seeck's text of all the *Relationes* with the exception of 3 and 11 is derived from three sources: two manuscripts and the *editio princeps*. The manuscripts are *T* (codex Tegernseensis or, as it is now called, Monacensis 18787, 11th

---

[1] Aug. *Ep.* 15 (A.D. 390) refers to a shortage of papyrus, but it may have been local and temporary.

cent.) and *M* (codex Mettensis 500, 11th cent.). From a study of the variations between them Seeck regards these manuscripts as representing independent traditions; there is nothing to recommend one as against the other except merit in the given passage. The *editio princeps* was by Sigismund Gelenius, published at Basle in 1549. Comparison of variations shows that the *editio* relied neither on *T* nor on *M*, but on an unknown manuscript. If Gelenius had consulted either *T* or *M*, he would not have included some of the errors which he did. At the same time he sometimes preserves a good reading, and Seeck has a high opinion of his ability to conjecture sensibly.

For 3 there is an additional source. Ambrose obtained a copy of 3 from the Emperor Valentinian II so that he could reply to it, and the *Relatio* and Ambrose's two letters in reply were published together as a Christian manifesto. That is why later these letters of Ambrose were sometimes printed with the *Relationes* and 3 was included in Ambrose's works. The variants are not of great significance, but Ambrose's copy of 3 shows that it was sent to Valentinian and not, as the text of Symmachus says, to Theodosius. Finally, 11 is included in a medieval *florilegium* (A.D. 1510) which contains a collection of letters and among them some of the *epistolae* of Symmachus.

Thus the task of producing a text of the *Relationes* is remarkably light compared with the labour which has to be expended on many other authors. Only three independent sources have to be examined; for 3 and 11 four. As will be seen in the notes Seeck introduces a few emendations made by himself and by Meyer and Gelenius, and he fills in some lacunae.

In his preface Seeck draws up lists of readings for the purpose of comparing the manuscripts, and the *apparatus criticus* below his text gives a full record of variants. The brief account of the manuscripts given above is derived from his preface.

INTRODUCTION

Editions

1. *Symmachi epistolarum libri decem*, ed. Franc. Juretus, Paris, apud Nicolaum Chesneau, uia Jacobaea, sub quercu uiridi, 1580. *Notae* discuss selected readings.

2. *Symmachi epistolae*, ed. Jac. Lectius, Lyons, 1587, 1598, 1601. In the 1587 edition he gives his own recension, a short index, and Juretus' notes. Marginal notes refer to other readings and to *CTh*.

3. *Susiana ad Symmachum*, ed. J. Gurlittus, Hamburg, 1816–18. Notes left by Suse, born 1781 at Hamburg, where he practised law; he spent his 'otium a multis eheu! ludis conviviis aliisque vitae oblectamentis impensum in veteribus scriptoribus diligenter legendis'; he died when thirty years old, 'febri nervosa subito correptus'. The notes on Symmachus were published after his death. They are not long and discuss readings and subject-matter.

4. *Quinti Aurelii Symmachi v.c. cons. ordinarii et praefecti urbi epistolarum lib. x castigatissimi, cum auctuario duo libelli S. Ambrosii episc. ad Valentinianum imper., eiusdemque epistola ad Eugenium cum miscellaneorum lib. x notis nunc primum editis*, A. Fr. Iur. D., Parisiis ex typographia Orriana. Anno Christiano 1604. Cum privilegio regis.

   This is Juretus' second edition which held the field for 279 years. The notes are rather sparse: they give reff. to the *CTh*. (but by title only) and to writers often later than Symmachus. But there is little attempt to explain the circumstances of the *Relationes* and still less to explain the argument of them.

5. *Symmachi epistolae*, ed. Gaspar Scioppius, Moguntiaci, 1608.

6. *Symmachi Epistulae*, ed. John Philip Pareus, Neapoli Nemetum, 1617 and later. Contains no notes and no discussion of readings. It includes a short life of Symmachus by Gothofredus. *Electa*, in 101 pp., groups notable thoughts in the letters under a large number of headings arranged alphabetically. *Calligraphia*, in no fewer than 320 pp., groups under very many headings phrases culled from the ten books, thus providing a storehouse for anyone wishing to write Latin in Symmachus'

INTRODUCTION

style. A *Lexicon*, in 168 pp., is very useful. The *Calligraphia* and *Lexicon* were published separately, but sometimes bound up with the letters. The *Electa* were present in all editions.

7. *Q. Aurelii Symmachi Relationes*, G. Meyer, Leipsig, 1872.

Text with very brief introduction on manuscripts and editions, and an excursus on the titles to the *Relationes*.

8. *Q. Aureli quae supersunt*, Otto Seeck, Berlin, 1883 (Monumenta Germaniae Historica), editio nova lucis ope expressa, 1961.

This splendid edition contains a text of the Epistles, *Relationes*, and Orations, in fact 'omnia quae supersunt', with apparatus criticus. The text is preceded by Chapters I 'de Symmachi orationibus', II 'de Symmachi relationibus', III 'de Symmachi epistulis', all of which deal with the manuscripts. They are followed by IV 'de Symmachi vita' which gives for the first time a detailed and documented life of Symmachus. These Chapters occupy pages i–lxxiii. Chapter V (pp. lxxiii–ccxi) is a 'chronologia et prosopographia Symmachiana', in which the arguments for dating the individual letters etc. are marshalled and the careers and the lives of the men concerned are constructed; this is a most valuable chapter. These chapters are equipped with footnotes in which the relevant citations are often given in full. The text is followed by indexes: I, the writings listed in chronological order; II, names; III, authors cited by Symmachus or in the introductory chapters. This monument of learning, industry, and insight, which put Symmachan studies on a new basis, was made possible by the publication of *CIL*. The *Codex Theodosianus*, in Gothofredus' remarkable edition, was already available; inscriptions gave reality to its formal pronouncements and life to innumerable men hitherto names; they enabled temporal and logical order to be imposed upon unrelated data. The contribution of this edition to the history of the later Empire has been enormous.

Numeration

The numeration is different in various editions. Since Gothofredus' edition of the *Codex Theodosianus* and Lewis and Short, *Latin Dictionary* (and all books before 1872) use the numeration of Juretus, which regards the *Relationes* as

INTRODUCTION

part of Book X of the Epistles, the following table may be useful. (It will be seen that disturbance in the serial order arises because *Rel.* 3 is put much later by Juretus and Pareus.) Meyer and Seeck do not treat the *Relationes* as belonging to the Epistles.

Meyer and Seeck *Relationes*	Juretus *Ep. X*	Pareus *Ep. X*
1	15	22
2	16	23
3	54	61
4–40	17–53	24–60
41–9	55–63	62–70

Ep. X in Seeck comprises only two letters.

SELECT BIBLIOGRAPHY

SEECK, OTTO. *Q. Aurelii Symmachi quae supersunt*, Berlin 1883 (reprinted 1961).

CHASTAGNOL, A. *La Préfecture urbaine à Rome sous le Bas-Empire*, 1960.

—— *Les Fastes de la Préfecture de Rome au Bas-Empire*, 1962.

MACGEACHY, J. A. *Q. Aurelius Symmachus and the Senatorial Aristocracy of the West* (Diss. Chicago), 1942.

BLOCH, H. 'A new document of the last pagan revival in the West, 393–4 A.D.', *Harvard Theological Studies*, xxxviii (1938), 199 ff.

—— 'The pagan revival in the West to the end of the fourth century', in A. Momigliano (ed.), *The Conflict between Paganism and Christianity in the Fourth Century*, 1963.

BROWN, P. R. L. 'Aspects of the Christianization of the Roman aristocracy', *JRS* li (1961), 1–11.

—— *Augustine of Hippo*, 1967, esp. pp. 66–71.

CAMERON, A. 'The date and identity of Macrobius', *JRS* lvi (1966), 25–38.

MATTHEWS, J. F. 'The historical setting of the "Carmen contra paganos"', *Historia*, xix (1970), 464–79.

INTRODUCTION

MATTHEWS, J. F. 'Symmachus and the *magister militum* Theodosius', *Historia*, xx (1971), 122–8.

—— *Western Aristocracies and the Imperial Court, 365–425* (forthcoming).

ROBINSON, D. M. 'An analysis of the pagan revival of the late 4th century with special reference to Symmachus', *Trans. American Philological Association*, xlvi (1915), 87–101.

BOISSIER, G. *La Fin du paganisme*, 3rd edn., 1898, ii. 155 ff., 262 ff.

DILL, S. *Roman Society in the Last Century of the Western Empire*, 1899 (Meridian, 1958).

DUDDEN, F. HOMES. *The Life and Times of St. Ambrose*, 1935.

JONES, A. H. M. *The Later Roman Empire 284–602*, 1964.

KIDD, B. J. *A History of the Church to A.D. 461*, 1922.

PIGANIOL, A. *L'Empire chrétien 325–395*, 1947.

JONES, A. H. M., MARTINDALE, J. R., and MORRIS, J. *The Prosopography of the Later Roman Empire*, 1970.

TABLE OF DATES

WESTERN EMPIRE	EASTERN EMPIRE
364 Valentinianus I	364 Valens
375 Gratianus	
	378 Theodosius
383 Valentinianus II 384–5 Symmachus *praefectus urbi* (Maximus 383–8, in Italy 387–8)	
392 Theodosius (Eugenius 392–4) 395 Honorius	395 Arcadius
	408
423	

FAMILY TREE OF THE EMPERORS

```
                    Gratianus
                        |
        ┌───────────────┴───────────────┐
Marina Severa = Flavius VALENTINIANUS I = Justina      VALENS         Flavius Theodosius = Thermantia
                b. 321 d. 375                       b. 328 d. 378                  |
        |               |                                          ┌───────────────┴───────────────┐
        |          VALENTINIANUS II                           Galla = THEODOSIUS I = Aelia Flavia Flacilla
        |          b. 370 (371) d. 392                               b. 346? d. 395
   GRATIANUS                                                         |
   b. 359 d. 383                                          ┌──────────┼──────────┬──────────┐
                                                  Galla Placidia  ARCADIUS  HONORIUS    Pulcheria
                                                                            b. 384 d. 423
```

26

RELATIONES

1

Symmachus thanks Valentinian II for conferring the prefecture of the city on him in July 384. He was about 44 years old and Valentinian 13 or 14. This dispatch thanks the Emperor of the West, 2 thanks the Emperor of the East; thus the idea that the prefecture was a joint appointment was maintained.

D. N. VALENTINIANO SEMPER AVG. SYMMACHVS V. C. PRAEFECTVS VRBIS

Quieto mihi et iam pridem a desideriis honorum remoto praefecturam multis cupitam sponte tribuistis. ago gratias tot bonorum erga me principum voluntati, sed intellego, quanto plus sollicitudinis habeat magistratus, qui ex iudicio, quam qui ex gratia venit. ille enim ut meritis datus spem sui debet aequare, iste ut per beneficium quaesitus a periculo *ex*pectationis* alienus est, domini imperatores. 2. quis ergo me huic honori parem faciet? scilicet vestra clementia, cuius interest, ne temere existimer electus; mihi ad conscientiam satis est non adfectasse publicam curam. iam qualis inveniar, in manu temporum est; bonos enim magistratus favor principum facit semperque de moribus vestris virtutes iudicum fluunt. 3. facite, ut omnes intellegant, si forte desit rectoribus integer vigor et iusta conscientia, hominis culpam esse non saeculi. non sum voti inmodicus, cum honorem meum commendo auctoribus suis. quantum est enim, quod ego numini vestro ago gratias? facite, ut vobis etiam res p. pro me grata sit.

---

* Italics in the text indicate conjectures made by Juretus, Meyer, Seeck, and others. When a lacuna is indicated, the words suggested by Seeck to fill the lacuna are recorded in these notes in order to show what has been rendered in the English translation.

TO OUR LORD VALENTINIAN, FOR EVER AUGUSTUS, GREETING FROM SYMMACHUS, OF THE DISTINGUISHED ORDER OF SENATORS PREFECT OF THE CITY[1]

I live a retiring life:[2] I have long ceased to hanker after public office; yet you of your own volition have accorded to me the prefecture, which is the ambition of many. I render thanks for the good will which so many imperial rulers bear to me; I realize that much more responsibility attaches to an office conferred by deliberate choice than to one granted as a favour. 2. The first, being conferred for merit, must live up to the hopes reposed in it; the second, obtained as a present, is free from the hazardous task of satisfying expectation, my Lords Emperors. Who then will make me equal to this office? Naturally, your Clemencies; for it is to your interest to see that people should not think I have been selected by random choice; as for myself it is enough for me to know in my heart that I have not aspired to public responsibility.[3] The kind of prefect I shall prove to be rests in the hands of circumstances; good magistrates are made by the good favour of Emperors; at all times it is from your high qualities that the virtues of magistrates flow. 3. Make everyone understand that if by any chance rulers should fail in unremitting energy or in a sense of integrity, the fault is in the man and not in the times. I am not asking too much of you if I entrust this office of mine to those who are its authors. After all, it is of little moment that I should render thanks to your Divinities; it is for you to see to it that the state too is grateful to you for me.

---

[1] For the form of address see p. 15.

[2] His last appointment was as proconsul of Africa from 373 to September 374, though he did not leave the province till spring 375. Behind Symmachus' unwillingness to take office, often expressed in the *Epp.* (e.g. 7. 50), lay a tradition, perhaps an affectation, of *otium* as a desirable way of life.

[3] Cf. **21.** 4.

2

A similar letter to Theodosius, who was 38 years old, while Arcadius was probably 7.

D. N. THEODOSIO SEMPER AVG. SYMMACHVS V. C. PRAEFECTVS VRBIS

Olim me, ut res indicat, cogitationes numinis vestri secundo favore respiciunt: neque enim aliter imperatoribus nihil temere praestantibus inter primos aut primus occurrerem. dilatus ergo hactenus mihi cum re p. videor, quae ubi in longinquas imperii partes maiestatis vestrae curam vocavit, repperit apud vos meditata iudicia, ddd. nnn. imperatores. 2. angustum est igitur, ut aeternitati vestrae pro solo honore, quem cepi, gratias agam: praefectos saepe fecistis et inmensa aetate facietis, sed quos adsiduitas et usus ingesserit; me dudum proconsularem virum cedentem iam diu potentium moribus ante capere magistratum quam expectare voluistis. nunc vos oro atque obsecro, ut favore perpetuo factum vestrum iuvetis. amabile est praeesse civibus, sed placere difficile. multum enim sibi ....[a] et inter cognitos semper dura constantia est. 3. quid, quod plerumque evenit, ut ....[b] aliqui longae potentiae usu iam nesciant? honorem meum non deseruerint, qui dederunt; ego enitar, ut potero, ne clementiam vestram fefellisse de me prior fama videatur: vestri numinis erit communem causam tueri. nam in bonis magistratibus maiorem gloriam quaerit temporum fama quam iudicum.

[a] licentiae usurpant *Seeck* [b] aliis obsequia praestare *Seeck*

TO OUR LORD THEODOSIUS, FOR EVER AUGUSTUS, GREETING FROM SYMMACHUS, OF THE DISTINGUISHED ORDER OF SENATORS, PREFECT OF THE CITY

For a long time, as events show, your Divinities, in making your plans, have regarded me with goodwill and favour. Otherwise my name would not have been the first, or indeed among the first, to occur to Emperors who put forward nothing without reflection. In my somewhat late appointment to office I seem to share the experience of the state; for it invites the attention of your Majesties to a problem in a distant part of the Empire and then finds that the decisions you take have long been thought out in advance, my Lords Emperors. 2. Thus I should restrict my thanks unduly if I thanked your Eternities only for the office you have bestowed on me. You have appointed many prefects, and in long lapse of time will appoint more; but they have been men recommended to you by their industry and experience. All this time I have been of proconsular rank, yielding to the ways of men who have long been powerful: yet you have willed that I should take a magistracy even before I had begun to expect it. I beg and beseech that your abiding good will should reinforce what you have done. It is gratifying to have charge of one's fellow-citizens: to please them is difficult. [For they claim for themselves too much freedom] and it is always difficult to be firm with people known to one. 3. Again, it often happens that some men who have long enjoyed power do not know [how to give to others the obedience due from them]. Do not let it be said that those who bestowed this office failed to support it: I shall do my best to ensure that my previous reputation shall not be thought to have betrayed your graciousness to me. It is or your Divinities to guard a cause which we now share. For a worthy tenure of office reflects more glory on the times than on the holder.

3

Date of dispatch, summer.

After the battle of Actium Augustus set up in the senate-house a statue and Altar of Victory to celebrate not so much a naval victory as the triumph of the Roman spirit over all that threatened to destroy it (Cassius Dio 51. 22). This altar became a symbol of the official state-cults as a whole, and as such it figures in the religious struggle of the fourth century. The imperial policy may be summarized thus:

Constantius removed the altar, but allowed all other cults to continue. Julian restored it, but in general his restoration of paganism failed. Valentinian I and Valens left it in position, but on the whole compromised, restoring some property to the temples and permitting sacrifice but forbidding nocturnal rites (§ 3). The effective break between the Roman state and Roman religion was brought about by Gratian: he removed the altar and refused to become Pontifex Maximus. He diverted the revenues of the priesthoods to public funds, seized the property which furnished the revenues, and deprived priests and temple officials of the privileges (*munera*) to which they had been entitled.

To Symmachus and his friends the loss of financial support was serious enough. But more important to them was the dissociation of state and state-religion: they believed that if the cults were not officially recognized they ceased to be valid and lost their efficacy. Four attempts were made at resistance.

1. Symmachus was sent by the senate to plead with Gratian: he was refused audience (§ 1).

2. **3** was composed by Symmachus in the name of the senate, which may have had a pagan majority, and was sent to Valentinian. Ambrose, bishop of Milan, heard that the dispatch had been sent and without having seen it sent a letter to Valentinian (*Ep*. 17) asking to see the full text: it was a harsh and bullying letter to a boy and threatened excommunication if the Emperor yielded. After receiving the text he wrote again (*Ep*. 18) taking Symmachus' points one by one and rebutting and ridiculing them, though admitting the high character of Symmachus and admiring

his eloquence. The pagan party had hoped for success since shortly before the Emperor had required Symmachus to punish those who had despoiled the temples.

3. Symmachus wrote to Theodosius, probably in 391, but without success.

4. The fourth attempt was made in 392. Eugenius made grants from his private funds to leading senators who could use them for religious purposes (Ambr. *Ep.* 57). The success was momentary: Eugenius was defeated by Theodosius who proscribed paganism.

Some twenty years later Prudentius wrote two books in hexameters called *contra Symmachi orationem*. He pays high tribute to Symmachus as a good man and a good orator. In the first he discourses on the folly of superstition and on the inanity of trying to keep alive something already dying: in the second he deals with some of Symmachus' points, even paraphrasing passages.

D. N. THEODOSIO SEMPER AVG. SYMMACHVS V. C. P. V.

Vbi primum senatus amplissimus semperque vester subiecta legibus vitia cognovit et a principibus piis vidit purgari famam temporum proximorum, boni saeculi auctoritatem secutus evomuit diu pressum dolorem atque iterum me querellarum suarum iussit esse legatum.

cui ideo divi principis denegata est ab inprobis audientia, quia non erat iustitia defutura, ddd. nnn. imperatores. 2. gemino igitur functus officio et ut praefectus vester gesta publica prosequor et ut legatus civium mandata commendo. nulla est hic dissensio voluntatum, quia iam credere homines desierunt, aulicorum se studio praestare, si discrepent. amari coli diligi maius imperio est. quis ferat obfuisse rei publicae privata certamina! merito illos senatus insequitur, qui potentiam suam famae principis praetulerunt: noster autem labor pro clementia vestra ducit excubias. cui enim magis commodat, quod instituta maiorum, quod patriae iura et fata defendimus, quam temporum gloriae? quae tunc maior est, cum vobis contra morem parentum intellegitis nil licere.

3. repetimus igitur religionum statum, qui reip. diu profuit.

TO OUR LORD THEODOSIUS, FOR EVER AUGUSTUS, GREETING FROM SYMMACHUS OF THE DISTINGUISHED ORDER OF SENATORS PREFECT OF THE CITY[1]

When the distinguished Council of the senate, which is always devoted to you, realized that law had gained the upper hand over wickedness[2] and when it saw that the evil reputation of recent times was being purged away by good Emperors, then it at once followed the powerful precedent set in a happy era; it got off its chest the indignation it had long repressed and once again it instructed me to convey its complaints.

In the reign of the late Emperor[3] audience with him was refused to me by unscrupulous officials for the precise reason that justice was likely to prevail, my lords and Emperors. 2. And so I act in a double capacity; as your prefect of the city I am transacting public business, as an envoy I present the message of my fellow citizens. No disagreement of purpose is involved in this matter; for men no longer believe that they gain greater support among court officials if there is a difference of opinion about the matter of a petition. To be loved, to be held in veneration and affection are greater things than to rule. It would be intolerable if private rivalries should be found to have conflicted with the interest of the state. And so the senate is right to proceed against anyone who has preferred his own power to the good name of the Emperor; in fact it is our task to watch over your Clemencies, like a sentry on duty. It is the honour of the times which has most to gain from our defence of our traditional institutions, of our country's rights and destinies; and that honour is all the greater at this moment because you understand that you have no power to do anything contrary to the precedents set by your parents.

3. That is why we ask you to give us back our religious

---

[1] This address is wrong. The *Relatio* was addressed to Valentinian, Theodosius, and Arcadius, and sent to Valentinian (Ambr. *Ep.* 57. 2, 17. 12).

[2] This may refer to the success of Praetextatus in obtaining a rescript ordering Symmachus as *praefectus urbi* to bring to justice Christians who had stolen treasure and material from the temples for private use, cf. **21**. 3.

[3] Gratian.

certe dinumerentur principes utriusque sectae utriusque sententiae: pars eorum prior caerimonias patrum coluit, recentior non removit. si exemplum non facit religio veterum, faciat dissimulatio proximorum. quis ita familiaris est barbaris, ut aram Victoriae non requirat! cauti in posterum sumus et aliarum rerum ostenta vitamus. reddatur saltem nomini honor, qui numini denegatus est. multa Victoriae debet aeternitas vestra et adhuc plura debebit: aversentur hanc potestatem, quibus nihil profuit; vos amicum triumphis patrocinium nolite deserere. cunctis potentia ista votiva est; nemo colendam neget, quam profitetur optandam. 4. quodsi huius ominis non esset iusta vitatio, ornamentis saltem curiae decuit abstineri. praestate, oro vos, ut ea quae pueri suscepimus, senes posteris relinquamus. consuetudinis amor magnus est; merito divi Constantii factum diu non stetit. omnia vobis exempla vitanda sunt, quae mox remota didicistis. aeternitatem curamus famae et nominis vestri, ne quid futura aetas inveniat corrigendum. 5. ubi in leges vestras et verba iurabimus? qua religione mens falsa terrebitur, ne in testimoniis mentiatur? omnia quidem deo plena sunt nec ullus perfidis tutus est locus, sed plurimum valet ad metum delinquendi etiam praesentia numinis urgueri. illa ara concordiam tenet omnium, illa ara fidem convenit singulorum, neque aliud magis auctoritatem facit sententiis nostris, quam quod omnia quasi iuratus ordo decernit. patebit ergo sedes

institutions as they used to be when for so long they were of value to the state. Of course, we can list Emperors of either faith and either conviction: the earlier Emperors venerated our ancestral religious rites, the later did not abolish them.[1] If the religious attitude of the earlier Emperors did not set a precedent, let the policy of the blind eye adopted by more recent Emperors set a precedent! We are not on such good terms with the barbarians that we can do without an Altar of Victory! We are cautious in our attitude to the future and we avoid the portents incidental to change. If honour is refused to the divinity herself, at any rate let it be duly given to the divine name. Your Eternities owe much to victory and will owe more. Let those reject her powerful aid who have never received a benefit from it; do you refuse to abandon a patronage so ready to bring you triumphs! Everyone prays for power of that kind; no one should deny that such power is to be venerated if he admits that it is desirable.

4. If to reject such a good omen (*as the restoration of an Altar of Victory would have been*) was not right, at any rate it would have been becoming to refrain from laying hands on the ornaments of the senate-house. Grant, I beg you, that what in our youth we took over from our fathers, we may in our old age hand on to posterity. The love of established practice is a powerful sentiment; the action of the late Emperor Constantius quite rightly did not stand good for long. You should not adopt any precedent which you have discovered to have been quickly set aside. We are safeguarding the perpetuity of your good name, ensuring that future ages will not find it necessary to reverse your measures.

5. Where else are we to take the oath of allegiance[5] to your laws and ordinances? What religious sanction is going to deter the treacherous from giving false evidence? Admittedly everywhere is full of God and nowhere is safe for perjurors; but to have it borne in upon you that you are in the presence of divine being is a powerful influence to make you fear to do wrong. That altar holds together the harmony of all as a group and that same altar makes its appeal to the good faith of each separately, and nothing gives more authority to the proceedings of the senate than the feeling that all its measures are passed by a body of men acting, as it were, on oath. Is a perjured witness to have ready

---

[4] See introductory note: 'later' means Valentinian I especially.

[5] Taken at sessions of the senate.

profana periuriis, et hoc inclyti principes mei probabile iudicabunt, qui sacramento publico tuti sunt?

6. sed divus Constantius idem fecisse dicetur. cetera potius illius principis aemulemur, qui nihil tale esset adgressus, si quis ante se alius deviasset. corrigit enim sequentem lapsus prioris et de reprehensione antecedentis exempli nascitur emendatio. fas fuit, ut parens ille clementiae vestrae in re adhuc nova non caveret invidiam: num potest etiam nobis eadem defensio convenire, si imitemur, quod meminimus inprobatum? 7. accipiat aeternitas vestra alia eiusdem principis facta, quae in usum dignius trahat. nihil ille decerpsit sacrarum virginum privilegiis, replevit nobilibus sacerdotia. Romanis caerimoniis non negavit inpensas, et per omnes vias aeternae urbis laetum secutus senatum vidit placido ore delubra, legit inscripta fastigiis deum nomina, percontatus templorum origines est, miratus est conditores, cumque alias religiones ipse sequeretur, has servavit imperio.

8. suus enim cuique mos, suus ritus est: varios custodes urbibus cultus mens divina distribuit; ut animae nascentibus, ita populis fatales genii dividuntur. accedit utilitas, quae maxime homini deos adserit. nam cum ratio omnis in operto sit, unde rectius quam de memoria atque documentis rerum secundarum cognitio venit numinum? iam si longa aetas auctoritatem religionibus faciat, servanda est tot saeculis

access to a place no longer consecrated, and to such a measure will my noble Emperors give their considered approval who are themselves protected by a general oath of loyalty?

6. It will be urged, however, that the late Emperor Constantius did exactly this. Let us imitate all his other actions rather than this, for he would never have approached such a course if anyone had made this mistake before him. The mistake of a predecessor offers a lesson to a successor, and from the adverse criticism of an earlier instance is derived the readiness to make correction. It was perfectly right for your Clemencies' ancestor[6] to take no precautions against giving offence, for the matter had never arisen before; but the same line of defence is not open to us if we copy a measure which we remember to have been condemned. 7. Let your Eternities accept the other acts of this same Emperor and adopt them into practice, and so earn greater respect. He stripped away nothing from the privileges of the Vestal Virgins; he filled the priesthoods with men of noble birth, he allowed the cost of Roman ceremonies; he followed an overjoyed senate through all the streets of the Eternal City and, with no sign of disapproval in his face, he saw its shrines, he read the inscriptions giving the names of the gods on the pediments; he put questions about the origins of the temples; he showed his admiration for their founders;[7] though he himself followed other rites, he preserved established rites for the Empire.

8. Everyone has his own customs, his own religious practices; the divine mind has assigned to different cities different religions to be their guardians. Each man is given at birth a separate soul; in the same way each people is given its own special genius[8] to take care of its destiny. To this line of thought must be added the argument derived from 'benefits conferred', for herein rests the most emphatic proof to man of the existence of the gods. Man's reason moves entirely in the dark; his knowledge of divine influences can be drawn from no better source than from the recollection and the evidences of good fortune received from them. If long passage of time lends validity to religious observances, we ought to keep faith with so many centuries, we ought

---

[6] Constantius.

[7] For this visit see Amm. 16. 10. 4 f.

[8] Prudentius, *contra Symmachi orationem*, 2. 370-453 discounts the idea of a genius of Rome.

fides et sequendi sunt nobis parentes, qui secuti sunt feliciter suos.

9. Romam nunc putemus adsistere atque his vobiscum agere sermonibus: optimi principum, patres patriae, veremini annos meos, in quos me pius ritus adduxit! utar caerimoniis avitis, neque enim paenitet! vivam meo more, quia libera sum! hic cultus in leges meas orbem redegit, haec sacra Hannibalem a moenibus, a Capitolio Senonas reppulerunt. ad hoc ergo servata sum, ut longaeva reprehendar? 10. videro, quale sit, quod instituendum putatur; sera tamen et contumeliosa est emendatio senectutis. ergo diis patriis, diis indigetibus pacem rogamus. aequum est, quidquid omnes colunt, unum putari. eadem spectamus astra, commune caelum est, idem nos mundus involvit: quid interest, qua quisque prudentia verum requirat? uno itinere non potest perveniri ad tam grande secretum. sed haec otiosorum disputatio est; nunc preces non certamina offerimus.

11. quanto commodo sacri aerarii vestri Vestalium virginum praerogativa detracta est? sub largissimis imperatoribus denegetur, quod parcissimi praestiterunt? honor solus est in illo veluti stipendio castitatis: ut vittae earum capiti decus faciunt, ita insigne ducitur sacerdotii vacare muneribus. nudum quoddam nomen inmunitatis requirunt, quoniam paupertate a dispendio tutae sunt. itaque amplius laudi earum tribuunt, qui aliquid rei detrahunt; siquidem

to follow our forefathers who followed their forefathers and were blessed in so doing.

9. Let us imagine that Rome herself stands in your presence and pleads with you thus, 'Best of emperors, fathers of your country, respect my length of years won for me by the dutiful observance of rite, let me continue to practise my ancient ceremonies, for I do not regret them. Let me live in my own way, for I am free. This worship of mine brought the whole world under the rule of my laws, these sacred rites drove back Hannibal from my walls and the Senones from the Capitol. Is it true that I have been kept alive solely for the purpose of being reprimanded at my age? 10. I will see what kind of changes I think should be set on foot, but reformation of old age comes rather late and is humiliating.' And so we ask for peace for the gods of our fathers, for the gods of our native land. It is reasonable that whatever each of us worships is really to be considered one and the same. We gaze up at the same stars, the sky covers us all, the same universe compasses us. What does it matter what practical system we adopt in our search for the truth? Not by one avenue only can we arrive at so tremendous a secret. But this is the kind of case for men to put with time on their hands; at the moment it is prayers that we present to you, not debating arguments.[9]

11. The privileges of the Vestal Virgins have been taken away from them, and what does the benefit to your sacred treasury amount to? Is it to be said that generous emperors refused what parsimonious emperors granted? Their sole glory lies in their enlistment, so to speak, in the service of chastity; but the outward expression of their priesthood is held to be freedom from 'state-services',[10] very much as the bands they wear give distinction to their heads. All they ask for is the title of immunity, nothing more, for their poverty saves them from making any payments. In fact, anyone who deprives them of anything

---

[9] §§ 9 and 10 are paraphrased by Prud. 2. 83–90, and in 649–768 he makes Rome deliver the kind of oration which Symmachus ought to have made her deliver. Ambr. *Ep.* 18. 5 disposes of Symmachus' argument with 'En quales templa Romana praesules habent. Ubi tunc erat Iuppiter? An in ansere loquebatur?'

[10] Taxes and special levies on property, for example. Symmachus implies that the revenues of the six Vestal Virgins were trifling: he says nothing about other priesthoods. Prudentius mocks at the Vestal Virgins in 2. 1064–1132, Ambrose in *Ep.* 18. 12, 39.

saluti publicae dicata virginitas crescit merito, cum caret praemio. 12. absint ab aerarii vestri puritate ista conpendia! fiscus bonorum principum non sacerdotum damnis sed hostium spoliis augeatur! illud ten*u*e lucrum conpensat invidiam?

atqui avaritia in mores vestros non cadit. hoc miseriores sunt, quibus subsidia vetera decerpta sunt; etenim sub imperatoribus, qui alieno abstinent, quia resistunt cupiditati, ad solam detrahitur amittentis iniuriam, quod desiderium non movet auferentis. 13. agros etiam virginibus et ministris deficientium voluntate legatos fiscus retentat. oro vos, iustitiae sacerdotes, ut urbis vestrae sacris reddatur privata successio. dictent testamenta securi et sciant, sub principibus non avaris stabile esse, quod scripserint. delectet vos ista felicitas generis humani. coepit causae huius exemplum sollicitare morientes. ergo Romanae religiones ad Romana iura non pertinent? quod nomen accipiet ablatio facultatum, quas nulla lex, nullus casus fecit caducas? 14. capiunt legata liberti, servis testamentorum iusta commoda non negantur: tantum nobiles virgines et fatalium sacrorum ministri excludentur praesidiis hereditate quaesitis? quid iuvat saluti publicae castum corpus dicare et imperii aeternitatem caelestibus fulcire praesidiis, armis vestris, aquilis vestris amicas adplicare virtutes, pro omnibus efficacia vota suscipere, et ius cum omnibus non habere? itane melior est servitus, quae hominibus inpenditur? rem publicam laedimus, cui numquam expediit, ut ingrata sit.

15. nemo me putet tueri solam causam religionum: ex

actually contributes to their repute—if, as is true, a virgin sisterhood dedicated to the well-being of the state deservedly grows in esteem when reward is out of the question. 12. Let your treasury preserve its integrity and disregard savings of that kind. Let the exchequer under good emperors be enlarged by spoiling the enemy, not by mulcting priests; do the slender profits resulting from the latter course make up for the loss of popularity?

Greed is inconsistent with your character. Those who have suffered the withdrawal of your support are made all the more miserable by the following reflection: when emperors are in power who keep their hands off other people's property because they are devoid of cupidity, the exactions made by the state are not prompted by the motive of covetousness and the loss inflicted is confined solely to the victim. 13. But it was the wishes of dying men that bequeathed to virgins and servants of religion the lands which the exchequer now retains (*and so the dead also are wronged*). I beg you who are the priests of justice that the right to benefit from private bequests should be restored to the religious institutions of your city. Let men dictate their wills in peace of mind knowing that under emperors innocent of rapacity what they have written will stand for ever. Let the human race enjoy that kind of happiness and do you rejoice in it! Already the cause which I am pleading is a warning to dying men and they are anxious. Are we to take it that Roman religious institutions are outside Roman law? What title will this seizure of properties be given—properties which no legislation, no crisis has ever rendered void? 14. Freedmen receive legacies; proper benefits under the terms of wills are not refused to slaves; shall noble virgins and those who serve the religious institutions concerned with our destiny be the exceptions, excluded from the guarantees secured by rights of inheritance? What is the good of dedicating a holy society to the well-being of the state, of buttressing the eternity of the Empire with divine support, of associating friendly virtues with your arms and your regiments, of praying that all may go well with all men, if at the same time you do not deal justly with all men? On these terms is the slavery which hangs over mankind really better? We are damaging the state, for it never has done the state any good for it to be ungrateful.

15. Let no one imagine I am pleading the cause only of

huiusmodi facinoribus orta sunt cuncta Romani generis incommoda. honoraverat lex parentum Vestales virgines ac ministros deorum victu modico iustisque privilegiis; stetit muneris huius integritas usque ad degeneres trapezitas, qui ad mercedem vilium baiulorum sacra castitatis alimenta verterunt: secuta est hoc factum fames publica et spem provinciarum omnium messis aegra decepit. 16. non sunt haec vitia terrarum, nihil inputemus austris, nec rubigo segetibus obfuit, nec avena fruges necavit: sacrilegio annus exaruit. necesse enim fuit perire omnibus, quod religionibus negabatur. certe si est huius mali aliquod exemplum, inputemus tantam famem vicibus annorum: gravis hanc sterilitatem causa contraxit. silvestribus arbustis vita producitur et rursus ad Dodonaeas arbores plebis rusticae inopia convolavit. 17. quid tale provinciae pertulerunt, cum religionum ministros honor publicus pasceret? quando in usum hominum concussa quercus, quando vulsae sunt herbarum radices, quando alternos regionum defectus deseruit fecunditas mutua, cum populo et virginibus sacris communis esset annona? commendabat enim terrarum proventum victus antistitum et remedium magis quam largitas erat. an dubium est, semper pro copia omnium datum, quod nunc inopia omnium vindicavit?

religion; it is from acts of the kind I have described that all the disasters to the Roman race have arisen. The law of our fathers had honoured the Vestal Virgins and the servants of the gods by granting them means for a moderate livelihood and reasonable privileges. This gift stood intact right up to the time of those worthless dealers in small change who had diverted the subsidies of sacred chastity to pay the wages of common porters.[11] On this act followed a general famine;[12] the hopes of all the provinces were betrayed by a miserable harvest. 16. The lands were not at fault: we should not blame the winds; rust did not spoil the crops, nor did weeds choke the standing corn. It was blasphemy that dried up the year's yield; and it was bound to follow that all would perish, for religion was being denied its proper support. If there is on record any other example of such a catastrophe, I would agree that we should blame the vicissitudes of the harvest-seasons; but it is a really serious cause which brought about the kind of barrenness we have experienced. People were kept alive by eating the twigs of forest trees: the country folk were starving and flew to the oak trees (*to feed on acorns*). 17. What comparable disaster did the provinces have to endure when the public conscience provided food for the servants of religion? During the period when free corn was made available alike to populace and to holy virgins, was there any occasion when, to satisfy human needs, oak trees were shaken, when the roots of plants were torn up, when provinces came to the relief of each other, good harvests here supplying the deficiencies of bad harvests there? The public maintenance of the priests promoted the yield of the regions and was an insurance rather than an act of generosity. There is no doubt that the funds which the general scarcity of today has appropriated were always in the past granted to secure abundance for everyone.[13]

[11] The Vestals were granted free corn; if this grant were abolished, the *arca frumentaria* would profit, and so the dockers (*baiuli*) who handled the grain might be said to be paid by what was withheld from the Vestals.
[12] There had been a bad harvest in Africa in 383 (e.g. *Ep.* 4. 84) which affected the supply of corn to Rome. (Prud. ridicules famine as an argument (2. 910–1064), and Ambr. also (*Ep.* 18. 21 sq.).) But Symmachus is suggesting that the famine was sent by the gods because part of the revenues had been diverted to the *arca frumentaria*: the gods were retaliating in kind.
[13] Prud. 2. 282–369 expands this section and argues that the religion of Rome was not derived from the primitive customs of Roman ancestors.

18. dicet aliquis sumptum publicum denegatum alienae religionis inpendiis. absit a bonis principibus ista sententia, ut quod olim de communi quibusdam tributum est, in iure fisci esse videatur. nam cum res publica de singulis constet, quod ab ea proficiscitur, fit rursus proprium singulorum. omnia regitis, sed suum cuique servatis, plusque apud vos iustitia quam licentia valet. consulite certe munificentiam vestram, an adhuc publica velit existimari, quae in alios transtulistis. semel honori urbis delata conpendia desinunt esse tribuentium, et quod a principio beneficium fuit, usu atque aetate fit debitum. 19. inanem igitur metum divino animo vestro temptat incutere, si quis adserit, conscientiam vos habere praebentium, nisi detrahentium subieritis invidiam. faveant clementiae vestrae sectarum omnium arcana praesidia et haec maxime, quae maiores vestros aliquando iuverunt. vos defendant, a nobis colantur. eum religionum statum petimus, qui divo parenti numinis vestri servavit imperium, qui fortunato principi legitimos suffecit heredes. 20. spectat senior ille divus ex arce siderea lacrimas sacerdotum et se culpatum putat more violato, quem libenter ipse servavit. praestate etiam divo fratri vestro alieni consilii correctionem; tegite factum, quod senatui displicuisse nescivit. siquidem constat ideo exclusam legationem, ne ad eum iudicium publicum perveniret. pro existimatione est temporum superiorum, ut non dubitetis abolere, quod probandum est, principis non fuisse.

18. But someone will say that public money was refused to meet the cost of a religion which was not the state's. I hope good emperors will not entertain the view that what was in time past granted to individuals from public funds should be regarded as still in the jurisdiction of the exchequer. The state is composed of individuals and once a thing leaves the state it becomes the property of individuals once again. You rule everything but you also preserve for each his own possessions, and justice weighs more with you than lawlessness. Consult your own past generosity and ask it whether it wishes that things which you transferred into the possession of others should be regarded as still the property of the state. Moneys once and for all handed over to the good conscience of the state cease to belong to those who contributed them, and what from the outset was a free gift becomes by usage and passage of time something owed. 19. Anyone who maintains that, unless you accept the odium of removing a grant, you are in league with those who wish to make it, is trying to intimidate your divine minds with a fear that is groundless. Let the unseen guardian powers, the gods of all religious loyalties, be on the side of your Clemencies, and above all the powers which at various times have aided your forefathers. Allow them to defend you, allow us to worship them. We ask for that establishment of religious practices which preserved the Empire for the late father of your Divinities, which furnished a fortunate Emperor with legitimate heirs. 20. From his citadel among the stars that elder Emperor[14] looks down upon the tears of priests and believes that he has come under blame now that the custom which he himself was glad to preserve has been broken. Give your late brother[15] the satisfaction that a policy which was not really his has now been corrected; cover up an act which he did not realize had displeased the senate—for indeed it is agreed that the delegation sent to him by the senate was denied access to his presence with the deliberate purpose of keeping him ignorant of public opinion. It would do much to redeem the reputation of earlier times if without hesitation you cancelled a policy of which indubitably the Emperor was not the author.

[14] Valentinian I.   [15] Gratian.

4

Gratian had ordered that the *praefectus urbi* should ride on official occasions in a *carruca*, a four-wheeled enclosed carriage. Symmachus protests against this pretentious innovation. (The matter is taken up again in **20**.) The protest is likely to have been made early in his term of office.

D. N. THEODOSIO SEMPER AVG. SYMMACHVS
V. C. P. V.

Quod apud germanum clementiae vestrae divum principem non sileremus, si eo res Romana frueretur, custodibus famae eius insinuo ea devotione, qua praefectum vestrum decet fidem praeferre blanditiis, domini imperatores. falso creditum est, quod urbanae fastigium potestatis peregrini ac superbi vehiculi usus adtolleret; haec ratio sola novum statutum benigno tunc persuasit ingenio, ut veterem magistratum dives pompa gestaret. 2. recusat istius modi decus honor sobrius, quem numquam paenitet sui; cui si quid patimur accedere, fatemur hactenus defuisse. itaque oculi quaerunt civitatis privati vehiculi nobilem modum et degenerem praefecturam populus Romanus existimat, quae posteriora traxit exempla. absit ut moderator urbis liberae atque ideo devotae tamquam Salmoneus Elius invehatur. nihil moramur externa miracula. 3. inritamentum superbiae Roma vestra non patitur memor scilicet bonorum parentum, quos Tarquinius fastus et ipsius Camilli currus offendit. nam tanto illi viro albentes quadrigae exilium triste pepererunt. at contra Publicolae decus tribuit inclinatio potestatis;

TO OUR LORD THEODOSIUS, FOR EVER
AUGUSTUS, FROM SYMMACHUS, OF THE
DISTINGUISHED ORDER OF SENATORS
PREFECT OF THE CITY

If the Roman world were still enjoying the presence of your Clemencies' brother the late Emperor,[1] I should not keep silence about the matter which I now venture to bring to your notice, who are the guardians of his good name: I do it with that sense of dedication which makes it fitting for a prefect to set loyalty before flattery, my Lords Emperors. It was believed, but quite wrongly, that the use of a foreign and pretentious type of conveyance[2] elevated the office of urban prefect to the height of distinction. At the time the kindly disposition of your predecessor was won over to this novel decision only by the desire that a richly furnished equipage should carry in procession the holder of a long-established magistracy. 2. But a temperate glorification of it which will regret no measure it takes rejects outward trappings of that kind; if we let anything be added to usual methods, we are admitting that up till now they were inadequate. The eyes of ordinary citizens look for a dignified form of conveyance, and the Roman people believes that a prefecture is on the decline if it has attracted to itself more recent standards of taste. God forbid that the ruler of a free city, dedicated to freedom, should be conveyed in a fashion more suited to Salmoneus of Elis.[3] We care nothing for marvels of display. 3. This Rome of yours does not tolerate anything likely to encourage pride: for it has not forgotten, as you know, its splendid ancestors to whom the arrogance of a Tarquin and the chariot even of a Camillus gave such offence; a great man though he was, his chariot drawn by

---

[1] Strictly, half-brother.

[2] Of Gallic origin? For *carruca* see Mart. 3. 62. 5, Plin. *Nat.* 33. 140, *Dig.* 21. 1. 38. 8; cf. Amm. 29. 6. 7. There is an illustration of it in *Notitia Dignitatum*, which is reproduced in A. Chastagnol, *Préf.*

[3] Salmoneus pretended to be Zeus; as he rode in his chariot torches were flung to imitate lightning and a noise like thunder was created (Apollod. 1. 9. 7).

submisit enim contioni civium consularem securem et honoris sui culmen infregit, ut libertatem civitatis erigeret. ergo moribus potius quam insignibus aestimemur. non culpamus novum beneficium, sed bona nostra praeferimus. submovete vehiculum, cuius cultus insignior est; illud maluimus, cuius usus antiquior.

four white horses procured for him a miserable exile.[4] On the other hand when Publicola lowered his own power the act brought him much honour; for he dipped his consul's axe in the presence of an assembly of the citizens and he diminished the pinnacle of his own glory in order that he might elevate the freedom of the citizen-body.[5] Let us then be held in regard for our character rather than for our trappings. We do not censure this novel concession, but we value more the good things we already have. Get rid of this conveyance; its array may be more spectacular, but we have always preferred the kind whose use is the more ancient.

[4] For the *superbia* of Tarquin see Liv. 1. 49–60. In 5. 23. 4, 5 Livy condemns the arrogance of Camillus' *quadriga* which equated a dictator with Jupiter.

[5] As consul Valerius Publicola lowered the *fasces* when he attended an assembly of the people, Liv. 2. 7. 6, 7. Plutarch, *Poplic.* 10, says the custom was observed in his day, cf. Vell. Pat. 2. 99. 3. The phrase is used metaphorically in Cic. *Brut.* 22, Plin. *Nat.* 7. 112.

Like other Roman writers Symmachus goes back to *exempla* from the early centuries of Roman history. Neither he nor they were deficient in historical knowledge or perspective, but these centuries contained the prototypes and precedents which had created Roman character and achievement and the history of them was almost sacred. Cf. **3, 15.**

5

Symmachus asks that senatorial rank may be granted to Celsus, a philosopher, together with exemption from the financial obligations of the rank.

D. N. THEODOSIO SEMPER AVG. SYMMACHVS
V. C. PRAEF. VRBIS

Inter praecipua negotiorum saepe curatum est, ut erudiendis nobilibus philosophi praeceptores ex Attica poscerentur; itaque nonnullos et*iam* auctoritas publica in usum nostrae urbis acci*v*it, domini imperatores. nunc vestri saeculi bonitas ultro optimatem sapientiae Romanis gymnasiis adrogavit. 2. siquidem Celsus ortus Archetimo patre, quem memoria litteratorum Aristoteli subparem fuisse consentit, iuventuti nostrae magisterium bonarum artium pollicetur, nullum quaestum professionis adfectans atque ideo dignus in amplissimum ordinem cooptari, ut animum vitiis avaritiae liberum dignitatis praemio muneremur. sunt huius rei exempla nobilia, quae prudens aemuletur imitatio. nam et Carneaden Cyrenaeum et Poenum Clitomachum Atheniensis curia societate dignata est, itidem ut nostri Zaleucum legum Locrensium conditorem civitate donarunt. 3. dignum est igitur aeternitate numinis vestri, Celsum genere eruditione voluntate laudabilem adiudicare nobilibus pignore dignitatis,

TO OUR LORD THEODOSIUS, FOR EVER
AUGUSTUS, FROM SYMMACHUS, OF THE
DISTINGUISHED ORDER OF SENATORS
PREFECT OF THE CITY

It has often been a major concern to ensure that teachers of philosophy should be invited here from Attica to educate members of noble families; accordingly the government itself has in the past summoned a number of such teachers to serve your city, my Lords Emperors. And now today the graciousness of your epoch has taken the step of claiming for the academies of Rome a high-ranking exponent of philosophical studies. 2. For Celsus,[1] the son of Archetimus, whom scholars, as they review the past, agree to be almost the equal of Aristotle, promises our young men his guidance in their liberal education; he is not trying to make money out of his profession; he deserves to be co-opted to the distinguished rank of senator precisely in order that we may recompense a mind free from the faults of avarice with the reward of high status. For this there are noteworthy precedents which it would be wise to copy and rival. The Council at Athens thought Carneades[2] of Cyrene and the Carthaginian Clitomachus[3] worthy of membership, just as our predecessors presented Zaleucus,[4] the lawgiver of Locri, with citizenship. 3. Therefore it would be worthy of the eternity of your Divinities to enrol among the nobility a man so estimable for his birth, learning, and goodwill as Celsus; it would be a token of his high standing with us; with it would go, naturally, the honorary status of a consul. We

[1] Nothing is known of Celsus or Archetimus.
[2] Founder of the New Academy at Athens and a member of the delegation of philosophers sent to Rome in 156–155 B.C. when he addressed the senate (Cic. *Luc.* 137, Gell. 6. 14. 8).
[3] He was instructed in Greek institutions by Carneades; he was a Sceptic and president of the Academy in 126 B.C.
[4] A very shadowy figure; he was said to be the lawgiver of Italian Locri in the seventh century; some said he never existed, Cic. *Leg.* 2. 15. The account given in Diodorus 12. 19. 3–21 is largely legendary.

cum praerogativa scilicet consulari, ne sumptum eius magis quam magisterium quaesisse videamur non sine avaritiae nota, si ab eo munia publica postulemus, qui spondet gratuita praecepta.

do not want to appear to have asked him to undertake financial expenditure⁵ rather than to direct studies; we should not avoid the stigma of avarice if we demanded from him services costing money when he promises instruction free of charge.

⁵ The 'services' to which a senator might be liable were the provision of Games (**8**), levies of recruits or horses in time of need, payment of the *aurum oblaticium* (**13**) and the *gleba*, a land-tax estimated on an annual return made to the census office (**46**).

6

This dispatch reminds the Emperor of his promise to provide Games. The tone is polite, but the meaning is that the people are becoming restive at the delay and Symmachus fears riots if the promise is not kept soon.

DD. NN. THEODOSIO ET ARCADIO SEMPER AVGG.

Praecipua[a] quidem beneficia numinis vestri populus Romanus expectat, domini imperatores, sed ea iam quasi debita repetit, quae aeternitas vestra sponte promisit; non quod sibi tribuenda diffidat—nusquam enim maior......[b] est quam in bonorum principum sponsione—, verum ne existimetur oblata fastidiose sperare, nisi instanter exegerit. 2. orat igitur clementiam vestram, ut post illa subsidia, quae victui nostro largitas vestra praestavit, etiam curules ac scaenicas voluptates circo et Pompeianae caveae suggeratis. his enim gaudet urbana laetitia, cuius desiderium pollicitatione movistis. 3. expectantur cotidie nuntii, qui propinquare urbi munera promissa confirment; aurigarum et equorum fama colligitur; omne vehiculum omne navigium scaenicos artifices advexisse iactatur. et tamen amor perennitatis vestrae acuit desideria plebis, non cupiditas ludicrorum. date igitur interim, quae petuntur, ut sit locus ceteris, quae sine fine tribuetis.

[a] *Seeck would prefer* perpetua [b] fides *Meyer*

TO OUR LORDS THEODOSIUS AND ARCADIUS
FOR EVER AUGUSTI

The Roman people looks for outstanding benefactions from your Divinities, but, my Lords Emperors, it now asks again for those which your Eternities voluntarily promised: for it regards them as owed. Not that it feels any doubt that they are to be rendered to it—for we can trust nothing with greater confidence than the undertaking of good emperors—but it does not wish, by not making an immediate demand, to give the impression of dissatisfaction with what is offered. 2. And so it begs that your Clemencies, after granting those subsidies[1] which your generosity has made towards our sustenance, should furnish also the enjoyments of chariot races and dramatic performances to be held in the circus and in Pompey's theatre.[2] The city delights in these entertainments and your promise has awakened anticipation. 3. Every day messengers are awaited to confirm that these promised shows will soon arrive at the city; reports on charioteers and on horses are being collected; every conveyance, every ship is rumoured to have brought in theatrical artists. Nevertheless it is affection for your Perennities, not avidity for entertainment, that has whetted the longings of the populace. Give for this moment what is asked of you so that in the future room may be left for all the other things which without limit you will bestow.

[1] The free or subsidized supplies of corn, wine, oil, pork, etc., to the city, see **14.** 3.
[2] Presumably the Circus Maximus; Pompey's theatre was finished in 53 B.C.; though often damaged by fire it remained till the sixth century.

7

The Emperors had sent a New Year's present to the senate, and Symmachus returns thanks on its behalf. It is not stated what the present was (§ 2 *munus*). In 15 Symmachus sends the senate's greetings, together with a present, to the Emperors. These two *Relationes* should be read together. The date is clearly December 384.

DD. NN. THEODOSIO ET ARCADIO SEMPER
AVGG. SYMMACHVS V. C. PRAEFECTVS VRBIS

Kalendas anni auspices, quibus mensium recursus aperitur, inpertiendis strenis dicavit antiquitas, domini imperatores Theodosi et Arcadi inclyti victores semper Augusti. huius instituti usum munificentiae festinatione praevertitis, seram putantes liberalitatem, quae statutis temporibus admovetur. felix me hercule saeculum, quo principes cohibere diu nesciunt tribuenda devotis, cum sibi debita cunctentur exigere! quid ergo primum, quid potissimum praedicem? 2. promptamne numinis vestri et celerem largitatem an circa absentes memorem diligentiam an quod sacrum munus auxistis honore verborum? dicam, ut res est, curasse clementiam vestram, ut tamquam coram locatus et adloquiis principum fruerer et augusta in ipsis donis ora venerarer. quando mihi eveniet expressa potius et viva gaudia capere de vobis? quantum veritatis est bonum, cuius species et imago mirabilis est! 3. ago igitur atque habeo gratias et meam vicem, qui solvendo non sum, caelestibus delego virtutibus. illae clementiam vestram dignis processibus munerentur; nos colimus, nos amamus, quod scitis omnibus rebus esse praestantius, qui ideo salutariter rem publicam regitis, ut haec sola mereamini.

TO OUR LORDS THEODOSIUS AND ARCADIUS
FOR EVER AUGUSTI, FROM SYMMACHUS, OF
THE DISTINGUISHED ORDER OF SENATORS
PREFECT OF THE CITY

The Kalends which herald the year, which open the returning cycle of the months, have been set apart by ancient custom for the giving of presents,[1] my Lords Emperors, Theodosius and Arcadius, glorious conquerors, for ever Augusti.[2] You anticipate the observance of this long-established practice by the speed with which you bestow your liberality, for you hold that generosity comes late if it is attached to fixed occasions. Happy indeed is the age in which rulers have long ceased to know how to curb the gifts they are to make to loyal subjects; for they are then slow to demand what is actually owed to them. What am I to praise first? What am I to praise especially? 2. Am I to make mention of the readiness, and indeed swiftness, of your Divinities' generosity? Of your painstaking care for your distant subjects? Of the distinction you added to your sacred gift by sending also a message? Let me declare—and it is the truth—that your Clemencies have made me feel that I was standing in front of you and enjoying conversation with Emperors and hearing with respect your august words at the moment of making the gifts. When will it happen to me to take delight in your manifest and living presence? How noble must the reality be when the reflected image is so admirable? 3. And so I express to you the gratitude I feel; the task of rendering any return I hand over to the heavenly powers of goodness, for I am unable to make payment. May they reward your Clemencies with every success, as you deserve! It is for us to revere you, to love you; you know that nothing is more excellent than to earn these sentiments, and these only; for your sound government of the state has this one aim.[3]

[1] For these presents (*strenae*) see Additional Note.
[2] The full formula would contain *ac triumphatores*, see **12. 1**.
[3] There is some similarity of language in **7** and **15**, e.g. *anni auspices* and *anni novi auspices*, *mensium recursus* and *annorum recursus*, *antiquitas* and *auctori Tatio rege*, but such greetings no doubt tended to be stereotyped.

8

Perhaps on a suggestion made by Symmachus, Theodosius had issued instructions to the senate to restrict undue expenditure on games, to draw up a procedure for the conduct of its business, and to submit to him exact regulations for Games; if he approved, he would confirm them by statute. Symmachus now sends detailed proposals to which this *Relatio* is a covering letter and asks for their endorsement. For date, probably July, see note on § 3.

DD. NN. THEODOSIO ET ARCADIO SEMPER
AVGG. SYMMACHVS V. C. PRAEFECTVS VRBIS

Omnium beneficiorum, quae tribuit potior fortuna subiectis, certa sunt tempora, domini imperatores, solae leges, quae in bonum commune procedunt, numquam patiuntur occasum. agit igitur divinis sanctionibus vestris gratias ordo reverendus etiam nomine posterorum, quibus res publica emendata tradetur. nam cum foeda iactatio senatorias functiones gravibus inpendiis obruisset, et moribus et sumptibus nostris sanitatem veterem reddidistis, ne aut inpares facultate collegas tenuis decoloraret editio aut per verecundiam viribus maiora conatos effusio inconsulta demergeret. 2. eiusdem praeterea orationis salubritate vetus dicendarum sententiarum forma reparata est, ne summum cuique decernendi locum non ratio munerum sed honorum fortuna praestaret atque id assensio ceterorum. vel invita sequeretur, quod ante omnes felicior censuisset. credimus igitur his remotis ad regnum suum redisse virtutes: in editionibus parsimonia, in senatu ordo retinebitur, nec se ostentabit opulentia semper bonis infirma temporibus.

3. superest ut ea, quae serenitas vestra patribus deliberanda legavit, cognito senatus consulto lex augusta confirmet. nullo enim dissentiente decretum est, quis modus censu*u*m semel

TO OUR LORDS THEODOSIUS AND ARCADIUS FOR EVER AUGUSTI, FROM SYMMACHUS, OF THE DISTINGUISHED ORDER OF SENATORS PREFECT OF THE CITY

Every blessing given by fortune (which is always more important to subjects of a ruler) is limited in time, my Lords Emperors; only the laws which march forward to serve the common good never set. And so to your divine Sanctions this venerable order of senators renders thanks also in the name of the posterity to whom shall be entrusted a state made better by your efforts. An ugly ostentatiousness had smothered the senate's official occasions beneath a burden of expenditure; but you have restored our former good sense both in our habits of mind and in the costs we incur. You were anxious that a modest provision of entertainment should not bring a stigma upon our colleagues whose resources are less and that unwise extravagance should not plunge into poverty those who for very shame attempted to do more than their financial strength warranted. 2. Moreover, thanks to this sound pronouncement of yours, the manner in which opinions are expressed in the senate has been given back its old shape, so that for each man priority in the order of expressing a judgement should depend not on considerations of the entertainments he had provided but on the offices he had been fortunate enough to hold, and that the rest should follow, even unwillingly, the judgement of the man who above all others had been blessed in this way. We believe therefore the way has now been cleared for the return of old virtues to their domain; economy in entertainments will be preserved, and due order in the senate; wealth, always insecure even in good times, will not parade itself.[1]

3. It remains that these matters which your Serenities have remitted to the senators for their consideration should be confirmed by an imperial law now that their decision has been ascertained.[2] For with no dissentient voice a resolution has now

---

[1] The need for the *perpetua firmitas* of a senatorial resolution to be confirmed by imperial statute is referred to in *CIust.* 1. 16. 1 (384).

[2] Restrictions may be seen in *CTh.* 15. 9. 1 (384), which forbids presents

aut saepius fungendis..........ᵃ mediocritas editionibus adplicetur, quae gladiatorio muneri et quae scaenicis ludis sumptuum temperamenta conveniant, quid libertatis habere mereatur praesentis expensio, quid damni absentium contumacia debeat experiri.

4. haec aeternitas vestra venerabilis cum senatui statuenda mandaret, referri ad se protinus imperavit, ut placita cunctis inmortali lege solidentur. iussis paruimus; expectamus oraculum, quo salutariter, ut vestro numini familiare est, patrum decreta firmetis, adiecta comminatione, si ullus aliquando ambitus haec vel illa corruperit, quae consilio caelesti pro ordinis dignitate sanxistis.

muneribus obnoxius sit, quae instruendis Seeck

been passed: it defines what assessment of wealth [shall make a man liable] for a single or for repeated entertainments, [what] limits shall be imposed on [the provision] of entertainments, how expenditure on gladiatorial shows and on stage-plays shall best be apportioned, what freedom of expenditure shall be allowed to one who stays in Rome to provide the entertainment, and what fine ought to be inflicted on anyone arrogant enough to absent himself.

4. Your venerable Eternities entrusted a decision on these matters to be determined by the senate, and ordered that they should immediately be referred back to you so that the resolution should be confirmed generally in a permanent law. We have obeyed your commands: we await a pronouncement to ratify the senate's decrees and to put things on the sound footing usual with your Divinities. We await too the addition of a stern warning to anyone led by ambition to modify these decisions or those which with divine prudence you have authorized to protect the dignity of our order.

of 'whole-silk' garments, gold coins, invitations written on ivory tablets (*diptycha*, see Dess. 1298–1312) to be kept as souvenirs, and in 6. 4. 25. Both were addressed to the senate at Constantinople by Theodosius, but it is unlikely that they were inspired by Symmachus.

9

This dispatch returns thanks for the lavish entertainments provided by the Emperor for the people: it reports that the senate has erected equestrian statues in honour of the father of Theodosius: it looks forward to the arrival of further supplies of corn. But its purpose is also to report Symmachus' opinion of the state of popular feeling, § 8. This feeling was signified by 'acclamations'—expressions of feeling for or against the Emperor or indeed on any matter of concern to him: they were not in any way official or formal, but were the more or less spontaneous outburst of a crowd gathering in such places as the Circus Maximus. It was the prefect's duty to report such acclamations, cf. 24: Chastagnol, *Préf.* 78 f. It is possible that the dispatch is intended to assure the Emperor that Rome remains loyal and will not support Maximus the usurper, cf. 43.

Symmachus later asks (43) that the erection of the statue in honour of Theodosius should be officially reported to the Eastern court of Theodosius, his son.

DD. NN. THEODOSIO ET ARCADIO SEMPER
AVGG. SYMMACHVS V. C. PRAEFECTVS VRBIS

Gratias beneficiis vestris agere pro urbe Roma ut officii probabilis ita insolentis audaciae est. nam neque ingentibus rebus verba conveniunt, et personam populi Romani nulla inplet oratio, domini imperatores. sed quia in talibus negotiis voti magis quam ingenii ratio versatur, non metuo inparis famam, dum fugio nomen ingrati.

2. urbem caelo et sideribus acceptam! cui bona terrarum omnium congeste praestavistis atque id praecipue vobis putatis accedere, quod Roma quaesiverit. recepimus veteris praerogativae fidem, securitatem. siquidem constat imperantibus vobis populi esse Romani, quidquid ubique generosum vel gignit natura vel informat industria. enimvero etiam posteris egregium dedistis exemplum: scient futuri ita demum adfluere publicas voluptates, si eas palatia non requirant. hoc est specimen animi continentis sibi negare, quod aliis deferatur, et laetitiam ceterorum propriis anteferre solaciis; hic usus bonos principes decet. namque aurium et oculorum fructus caducus est, largitatis aeternus. 3. alii triumphis suis haec dona servassent, ut posita lauru novis actoribus personarent Pompeiana proscaenia, ut pro captivis tetrarchis Indicae currum beluae praevenirent, ut equorum longus ordo instar gentium duceretur: vester triumphus Arsacidas post tergum revinctos et gazas victae Babylonis accipiet. in

TO OUR LORDS THEODOSIUS AND ARCADIUS
FOR EVER AUGUSTI, FROM SYMMACHUS, OF
THE DISTINGUISHED ORDER OF SENATORS
PREFECT OF THE CITY

To render thanks in the name of the city of Rome for your benefits is a laudable duty, but it is also an act of presumptuous audacity. No words match great deeds; no oration fulfils the role of the Roman people, my Lords Emperors. But, since in such matters regard is paid to intentions rather than to ability, I am not afraid of being thought unequal to the task, while at the same time I avoid being thought ungrateful.

2. The city has found favour with the heavens and the stars! To it you have made available the good things of all lands in heaped profusion; and you think it a special and an additional satisfaction that it is Rome that has obtained them. We have been given back the pledge of our ancient privileged position, namely security; for under your imperial rule it is taken for granted that whatever noble thing nature produces anywhere or the painstaking efforts of men fashion belongs to the Roman people. In fact, you have set an outstanding precedent to posterity; future generations will know that the stream of pleasures to be enjoyed by the public flows as abundantly as it now does, since the palaces do not need these. It demonstrates self-restraint to deny oneself something in order that it may be passed on to others, and to prefer the enjoyment of the rest of the world to one's own comforts; this is a practice most becoming to good emperors. The pleasure which comes through the ears and the eyes is fleeting: the pleasure given by generosity lasts for ever. 3. Others would have kept these gifts for their triumphs so that, abandoning the laurel-wreath of the victor, they might make the theatre of Pompey ring with the voices of the latest actors or that wild beasts from India might precede the triumphal chariot instead of captive chieftains, or that a long procession of horses might be led in to take the place of native prisoners; but in contrast your triumph will include Persians with hands tied behind them and treasure from conquered Babylon.[1]

---

[1] War with Persia had dragged on since the time of Julian and was not

magnos quippe animos non cadit adfectata iactatio. nescitis tribuenda differre; quidquid nationum famulatus obtulerit, statim publicum est.

4. merito vos senatus ac populus ore celebrat, devotione veneratur, amore conplectitur. mihi credite: arcana omnium pectorum possidetis, illa bonarum necessitudinum loca, quibus liberorum, quibus parentum inmoratur adfectio. et quia omne praemium, dum beneficiis vestris confertur, angustum est, invenit ordo amplissimus amabilem vicem, qua se gratum probaret. nam familiae vestrae et stirpis auctorem, Africanum quondam et Brittannicum ducem statuis equestribus inter prisca nomina consecravit, qui felici satu numen in imperium salutare progenuit. sic coluntur, quorum liberi ad bonum publicum nati sunt. 5. at vero populus imperialis munificentiae muneribus expletus in amorem vestrum prompta inclinatione concessit. qui ubi conperit meo praefatu, adfore dona publicorum parentum, portis omnibus in longinqua fusus erupit, feliciorem ceteros iudicans, qui primus bona vestra vidisset. ergo cum expectari munera principum soleant, nunc accita venerunt. praetereo illum diem, quo elefantos regios per conferta agmina equorum nobilium pompa praecessit; 6. malo fremitum Murciae vallis exponere atque illam quadrigarum distributionem, in qua sibi cum fortunatior videretur, cui electionem mox urna tribuebat, par vel potior erat, quem sors fecisset extremum.

For great minds do not admit of striving after ostentation. You are incapable of delaying the gifts you make: whatever the subject nations offer is immediately public property.

4. With good reason senate and people are loud in your praises, venerate you with all devotion, and enfold you in their love. Believe me, you occupy the secret recesses of all hearts, those places reserved for noble family affections wherein dwells the love of children for parents and of parents for children. And, because any return, compared with your benefactions, can be only slender, this noble order of senators has discovered a pleasant way of making a return to prove its gratitude. It has solemnly honoured with equestrian statues, and has thus enrolled among ancient names, the author of your family and line who was formerly general in Africa and in Britain;[2] he had the favour of fortune when he begat a Divinity to bring well-being to the Empire. This is the honour given to men whose children by their birth benefit the state. 5. Indeed the people, sated with the 'benefactions' given by imperial generosity, with a swift tilt of the balance have swung strongly in your favour. When it learnt from my preliminary announcement that the good things sent by the parents of the state would soon arrive, it broke from every gate and poured out for quite long distances, thinking that luck was with the man who was the first to see these good things. So, whereas these imperial benefactions are usually waited for, now they have arrived at call. I say nothing about the day when a procession led royal elephants through packed lines of magnificent horses; 6. I prefer to describe the noisy excitement in the valley of Venus of the Myrtles[3] when four-horse chariots were distributed; then anyone to whom the lot gave an early place in the choice (*of a chariot*) thought himself especially lucky; yet the man who drew the last place found himself at an equal or even at a better

concluded till about 386 by the partition of Armenia. Theodosius did not celebrate a triumph till 12 October 386. For other captives from the East see **47** (Sarmatians).

[2] Theodosius, father of the Emperor, a Spaniard and a Christian; rose to the highest military office as *magister equitum*; recovered Britain 367–9; sent to suppress the insurrection of Firmus in Africa 372–4; executed at Carthage 376 (Jer. *Chron.* 376) for reasons unknown to us. For Britain, Amm. 27. 8. 3 ff., 28. 3 ff.; for Africa, 29. 5. 1–55.

[3] Between the Aventine and Palatine hills, Liv. 1. 33. 5. Plin. *Nat.* 15. 121 identifies Venus Murcia (Aug. *C.D.* 4. 16) with Venus Myrtea.

quotiens sequenti primus invidit? dubia est optio, cum de similibus iudicatur. nec putetis istiusmodi voluptatem plebi Martiae parvam videri, cui delenimenta circensium finitimorum conubium praestiterunt, cui summus honor visus est, ut ovantes equorum dorsa gestarent, ut triumphantes currus inveheret. quare Victoria genti Romuleae familiaris clementiam vestram pro voto omnium muneretur. 7. fecistis ut urbs cana luxuriet in primam reducta laetitiam et ver illud quondam vigentis aetatis. audeo iam sperare potiora: mittetis etiam regiam classem, quae annonariis copiis augeat devotae plebis alimoniam. hanc vero in Tiberinis ostiis mixtus populo senatus excipiet; venerabimur tamquam sacras puppes, quae felicia onera Aegyptiae frugis invexerint. non sunt avara vota, quae saeculi excitavit humanitas: de exemplis venit ista fiducia; magna sumendo maiora praesumimus.

8. nunc legite senatus ac populi fausta suffragia, licet sciam, plus inesse animis, quam vocibus explicari, et quaedam libamina publici in vos amoris accipite. si parva adhuc dicta sunt, munerum vestrorum inputate miraculis; nam magnitudo stuporis locum multis plausibus non reliquit.

advantage. How often did the first drawer envy those who came after him? Choice is of doubtful value when the things about which one must decide are so alike. Do not imagine that pleasures of this kind mean little to the people of Mars; after all it was the attraction of their neighbours' horse-races that obtained wives for them,[4] and it was thought to be the highest honour that a man awarded an 'ovation' should ride on horseback and one awarded a triumph should be carried in a chariot.[5] Therefore may victory, the handmaid of the people of Romulus, recompense your Clemencies, as is the prayer of everyone. 7. Your efforts have made a city grey with age flourish again, have restored it to its original luxuriance and to the springtime of its earlier years of vigour. I hopefully await still better things; you are going to send a royal fleet to augment with plentiful supplies of corn the free maintenance of a devoted people. This fleet senate and people together will welcome in the entrances to the Tiber:[6] we shall revere as almost sacred the ships which will have brought in their bountiful cargoes of the crops of Egypt. It is not greed that inspires the desires which the humanity of the age has aroused; rather, the precedents you have set are the source of our confident expectations; because we have received so much we anticipate even more. 8. Now is the time for you to gather to yourselves the favour and approbation of senate and people, though I know that there is more in their hearts than is expressed in words; accept a preliminary outpouring of the public's affection for you. If, as I know, what I have said is brief, attribute it to the portentous nature of your benefactions; dumb amazement has left me little chance of applauding at length.

[4] Liv. 1. 9. 6.
[5] The difference between a triumph and an ovation is explained in Gell. 5. 6. 20, 21.
[6] Ostia and Portus Augustus.

10

Symmachus reports the death of Praetextatus, which occurred in December 384 (see also **11, 12, 21**. 5, 24). The whole city mourns him and he himself is so deeply shocked that he asks permission to resign his office (cf. **21**. 4). The dispatch must have been sent to Valentinian since he had made the appointment, and **11** seems to refer to this dispatch.

DD. NN. THEODOSIO ET ARCADIO SEMPER
AVGG. SYMMACHVS V. C. PRAEFECTVS VRBIS

Laetarum rerum index esse malueram, domini imperatores, sed ratio officii publici necessitatem mihi nuntii tristis inposuit. Praetextatus vester, Praetextatus bonorum, antiquae probitatis adsertor, invida sorte subtractus est, vir omnium domi forisque virtutum, in cuius locum vestrae quoque aeternitati, quae optimos novit eligere, nimis arduum est similem subrogare. 2. itaque summum sui in re publica desiderium magnumque civibus gratis reliquit dolorem. nam ubi primum Romae amarus de eo rumor increpuit, recusavit populus sollemnes theatri voluptates memoriamque eius inlustrem multa adclamatione testatus graviter egit cum livore fortunae, quod sibi inclytorum principum beneficia sustulisset. et ille quidem functus est lege naturae, nos vero socios animi sui vestrique iudicii tanto dolore confudit, ut otii remedium postulemus. 3. sileo cetera, quae me non sinunt praefecturam ferre patienter: vel haec una consortis

TO OUR LORDS THEODOSIUS AND ARCADIUS FOR EVER AUGUSTI, FROM SYMMACHUS, OF THE DISTINGUISHED ORDER OF SENATORS PREFECT OF THE CITY

I had preferred, my Lords Emperors, to bring good news, but considerations of public duty compel me to bring bad news. Praetextatus[1] whom you know well, Praetextatus, the champion of every good thing, of old-fashioned integrity, has been removed from us by a jealous fate—a man possessed of every high quality at home and abroad: even your Eternities, who know how to choose the best men, will find it very difficult to find a successor to compare with him. 2. In public life he has left behind him a deep longing for himself, and a bitter grief in the hearts of grateful citizens. When first the painful rumour about him spread abroad in Rome, the people refused the usual pleasures of the theatre; with loud shouts[2] it testified to his glorious memory and was angry at the malice of fortune which had robbed it of blessings given by renowned emperors. He indeed has fulfilled nature's law; as for ourselves (*Symmachus himself*), we shared his mind and your wise choice of him, and his death has so shaken us for sheer grief that we ask of you the consolation which a private life may bring. 3. I will not dwell on the other reasons which prevent me from sustaining my office as prefect with equanimity;[3] even

---

[1] Vettius Agorius Praetextatus, one of the leading figures of the period; champion of paganism. Married Aconia Fabia Paulina who dedicated a monument to him with a long inscription and a poem in praise of their forty years together, Dess. 1259; his career and priesthoods are given in detail. Quaestor, praetor, *corrector* of Tuscia-Umbria, *consularis* of Lusitania, proconsul of Achaea, *praefectus urbi* 367 to 20 September 368, praetorian prefect 384. He is the chief character in Macrobius' *Saturnalia*, where his religious beliefs are set out. Letters from Symmachus to him *Ep.* 1. 44–55; see also Amm. 27. 9. 8 ff., Jerome *Ep.* 23. 2, 3, Dess. 1258, 1259, 4003.

[2] An example of an 'acclamation', see **9** intro.; cf. Jerome *Ep.* 23. 3 for the universal mourning.

[3] Symmachus had lost an ally and felt himself isolated: moreover he found his office as prefect increasingly irksome. 'Other reasons' are suggested in **17, 22** (minor officials appointed against his wishes or without his knowledge), **23** (the enmity of the Vicar of Rome and of a barrister in his court), **21** (malicious charges of exceeding his duty), **34** (the attack on himself and his wife in 'the

amissio iusta est ad impetrandam vacationem. ament alii perpetuas potestates: mihi summus est fructus felicitatis, ut coram vestrum numen advenerer, intuear benign*a salu*tis meae sidera. hoc unum pro omnibus, quae praestitistis, exopto. simplex petitio est nec viam capessendi honoris adfectat; semel enim claru*e*rit nihil aliud esse, quod cupiam, cum supplex refuderim magistratum.

by itself the loss of a close associate would justify asking and obtaining release. Let others be enamoured of an unbroken succession of positions of authority. For me it is the peak of happiness to be in your presence and to venerate your Divinities, to gaze upon the stars whose benign influence has given me security. This is the one thing I crave for, in place of all that you have done for me. My request is single-minded: it is not looking for a path to further office. It will have become clear, once and for all, that there is nothing else I desire when at my own entreaty I have resigned my magistracy.

Orfitus affair'), **33, 39, 41** (the difficulty of administering justice when constitutions were inconsistent and courts overlapped).

11

It seems that Symmachus sent this letter by special messenger to anticipate **10,** which is the more formal of the two.

D. N. VALENTINIANO SEMPER AVG. SYMMACHVS
V. C. PRAEFECTVS VRBIS

Licet arbitrer litteras meas nuntiis aut rumore praeventas—quid enim fama potest esse velocius, domini imperatores?—ego tamen officii publici necessitate cogente excessum viri inlustris crudo adhuc dolore non sileo. Vettium Praetextatum veteribus parem virtutum omnium virum fata rapuerunt summo patriae gemitu, cui decus insigne praestabat. cuius ego laudes et iusta praeconia animi consternatione praetereo; neque enim locus est cuiusquam testimonio, cum vitae eius gloriam clementiae vestrae iudicia testentur, mortem celebrem dolor omnium fecerit.

TO OUR LORD VALENTINIAN, FOR EVER AUGUSTUS, FROM SYMMACHUS, OF THE DISTINGUISHED ORDER OF SENATORS PREFECT OF THE CITY

I think my dispatch to you may have been forestalled by messengers or by rumour—for nothing travels faster than report, my Lords Emperors. Nevertheless the demands of public duty prevent me from keeping silence about the death of a famous man, though my grief is still an open wound. Vettius Praetextatus,[1] the equal of the ancients, a man of every virtue, the fates have carried off amid the loud lamentations of his country to which he lent conspicuous distinction. Words of praise and the panegyric proper to him I must leave unsaid, for I am shocked at heart; indeed no room is left for anyone's witness to him, for your Clemencies' own judgements testify to the glory of his life, and universal mourning has made his death famous.

[1] See above, 10 n. 1.

12

Acting on behalf of the senate, Symmachus asks the Emperors to grant leave for statues of Praetextatus to be erected. Such statues would not only commemorate a man of outstanding services but would act as an incentive to others. The dispatch contains eloquent testimony to his qualities, but leaves it to the Emperors to render full tribute to him.

DD. NN. THEODOSIO ET ARCADIO SEMPER
AVGG. SYMMACHVS V. C. PRAEFECTVS VRBIS

Licet Vettius Praetextatus naturae lege resolutus sit, vivit tamen in memoria et amore cunctorum felicior civium lacrimis quam quisquam gaudiis suis, atque hoc uno punit invidiam, quod tantum ei mors ad gloriam contulit, ut huic quoque fortunae livor debeat invidere, domini imperatores Valentiniane Theodosi et Arcadi inclyti victores ac triumphatores semper Auggg. 2. nam praeter illum populi Romani inusitatum dolorem etiam senatus inpatiens dispendii sui solacium petit de honore virtutis vestrumque numen precatur, ut virum nostra aetate mirabilem statuarum diuturnitas tradat oculis posterorum, non quod ille praemia terrena desideret, qui gaudia corporis, etiam cum hominem ageret, ut caduca calcavit, sed quia ornamentis bonorum incitatur imitatio et virtus aemula alitur exemplo honoris alieni. hinc factum est, ut rusticis adhuc saeculis optimi quique civium manu et arte formati in longam memoriam mitterentur. atque utinam nihil huic decori facilitas

Praetextatus had achieved a very distinguished career (see above, 10 n. 1) and stood high in the regard of the court. This series of dispatches (11, 12, 21, 24) demonstrates the imperial respect for him but also his standing at Rome. *Ep.* 1. 44–55 convey the impression of a strong personality.

TO OUR LORDS THEODOSIUS AND ARCADIUS FOR EVER AUGUSTI, FROM SYMMACHUS, OF THE DISTINGUISHED ORDER OF SENATORS PREFECT OF THE CITY

Vettius Praetextatus in accordance with nature's law has been parted from life, but he lives in the affectionate memory of all, happier in the tears of his fellow citizens than another man in his own pleasures; indeed he avenges himself on a jealous fate in this simple way, that his death has so enhanced his glory that the malice of fortune ought to be jealous also of his death, my Lords Emperors, Valentinian, Theodosius, and Arcadius, renowned conquerors and winners of triumphs, for ever Augusti. 2. Not only is the people grieved beyond its wont, but also the senate intolerant of its loss seeks to derive some consolation for itself from paying honour to his high qualities. It entreats your Divinities that statues should perpetuate the image of a man remarkable in our age and hand it on to the gaze of posterity;[1] it entreats you thus not because he would long for any such earthly reward—for he, even when he was just an ordinary human being, spurned all physical pleasures as merely transitory—but because, if good men are given visible honours of this kind, others are stirred to copy them and, if a sample of someone else's honour is in front of them, a desire for goodness to rival his is fostered. This explains why even in the days when we were a rural community a likeness of all the best of our citizens was fashioned by skilful hand and handed down to be remembered by the ages.

[1] The Vestal Virgins also erected a statue to him, Sym. *Ep.* 2. 36. 2. See also Dess. 1261.

adulantium postea derogasset! quamvis paria non sint, quae dispari arte quaeruntur.

3. dignum est igitur, ut qui in pectoribus omnium manet, sit in ore populorum: ille semper magistratibus suis celsior; in alios temperatus, in se severus; sine contemptu facilis, sine terrore reverendus; cui si quod commodum successionis evenit, ad testatoris proximos mox revertit; qui nullius prosperis fractus est, nullius risit adversa; indecorae nescius largitatis ille, quem semper invitum secutus est honor, ...[a] cuius aequitati conterminus quisque limites suos credidit. 4. plura de eo vellem, plura deberem, sed clementiae vestrae testimonio cuncta servanda sunt; inlustrior enim laus est de caelesti profecta iudicio.

5. ergo ut probitatis patroni bona temporum vestrorum futuris quoque visenda proponite. certe ille est Praetextatus, quem iure consulem feceratis, ut fasti memores celebre nomen extenderent. aliis titulis fatalia damna reparate. abierit cum homine praemium, sed iudicium post hominem perseveret. probate casibus adversum gloriam nihil licere. nam quod meruit a civibus, singulare est, illud multis commune, quod perdidit.

[a] quaestus iniusti nescius *Seeck*

And I wish that flattery too ready to grant this honour had not detracted from it, though it is true that things obtained by an inferior art (*flattery*) are never equal in merit.

3. It would be fitting therefore that a man who abides in the hearts of all peoples should also find a place in their talk. He always towered above the magistracies he held; in dealing with other men he showed restraint, with himself he was stern; he was easy to approach, but was not therefore despised; he was to be regarded with respect but not with awe. If any benefit ever passed to him under the terms of a will, he immediately passed it back to the nearest kin of the testator. As he was never shattered by another's prosperity, so he was never amused by another's disasters. He was never guilty of dishonourably buying success; official position attended him often against his will; [he was never guilty of unfair gain:] to his sense of fairness all his neighbours believed they could trust their own boundaries.[2] 4. I should like to say more about him, I should like to feel it a duty to say more; but everything must be reserved for the testimony your Clemencies will give; for praise is all the more distinguished if it comes from a judgement inspired by heaven.

5. Therefore, as champions of integrity, hold up the good things of your times for all to see, future generations as well. Such as I have described is Praetextatus in very truth, the man whom you had rightly appointed consul,[3] so that the archives might preserve and exhibit so glorious a name. Make good the disastrous harm done by other insertions in the archives. A precious possession will have departed with the man, but after the man let your judgement of him endure. Prove that events can have no power in the face of glory. For what he has deserved from his fellow citizens for his services is unique; what he has lost is a loss common to man.

[2] For praise of Praetextatus see Amm. 22. 7. 6, 27. 9. 8.
[3] For the year 385.

13

The *decennalia* (sc. *vota*) was properly the celebration of the tenth year after the accession of an Emperor (nomination as 'Augustus' counting as accession). The observance of ten years dated from the time of Augustus whose renewal of power had been for ten years, 8 B.C., A.D. 3, 13. For the Emperors of 384 the most important element in the *decennalia* was the 'voluntary' contribution of the *aurum oblaticium* (called *oblatio* in **23.** 12) and the *aurum coronarium*. The second of these virtual taxes was paid by the

D. N. VALENTINIANO SEMPER AVG.
SYMMACHVS V. C. PRAEFECTVS VRBIS

Si divinae clementiae tuae merita cogitentur, nullae opes, quas aut natura sufficit aut fortuna circumfert, gratiam nostri erga te amoris aequabunt, sed ut mea fert opinio, publicum de optimo imperatore iudicium non est muneribus aestimandum. 2. senatus tamen promptus obsequii omnes officiorum partes ultro adripit, quibus indicatur adfectio, et salutare numen tuum precatur, ut in hac oblatione, quae nonnihil superioribus addidit, intellegas hoc esse curatum, ne sub te minus posse videamur. nam divis parentibus tuis ob decennium singulis minor summa decreta est; etiam divus frater mansuetudinis tuae, cum tertium lustrum aevi imperialis exigeret, parciore munificentia honoratus adseritur. nunc in amorem tuum studia nostra creverunt. nam mille sescentas auri libras decennalibus imperii tui festis devotus ordo promisit urbanis ponderibus conferendas, id est trutinae largioris examine.

decurions of towns, the first by the senate. The sum expected was apparently notified in advance (Sym. *Ep.* 2. 57) and it increased with each *decennalia*. Moreover the ten-year interval was by this time reduced to five years (§ 2 'third lustre'). Symmachus, in a dispatch which surely contains some irony (as does, for example, *CTh.* 12. 13), promises the contribution for Valentinian's *decennalia* celebrated on 22 November. For the Emperor's gift and Symmachus' thanks for it see **7**.

TO OUR LORD VALENTINIAN, FOR EVER AUGUSTUS, FROM SYMMACHUS, OF THE DISTINGUISHED ORDER OF SENATORS PREFECT OF THE CITY

If we reflect upon the deserts of your divine Clemency, the wealth which nature supplies or good fortune spreads round us will never equal the affection which we freely bestow upon you; on the contrary in my opinion the general verdict upon a good emperor can never be estimated by gifts. 2. Nevertheless the senate with ever-ready respect for you has taken the initiative in claiming for itself the complete discharge of its duties to you. In this way its affection is demonstrated, and it prays your beneficent Divinity to be aware that in this offering, which has added not a little to previous offerings, it has made every effort to avoid giving the impression that under your rule its resources are less than before. In honour of your late kindred a smaller sum was decreed on the occasion of the 'ten-year festival' of each of them.[1] Your Grace's late brother[2] is alleged to have had an even more miserly sum spent in his honour though he was completing the third lustre of his reign. But today our enthusiasm has grown into an affection for you. For, sixteen hundred pounds in gold your devoted senate has promised for the ten-year festival of your rule, and the pounds are to be compared with the weights kept in the city, that is to say, they are to be assessed by the pointer on much more generous scales.

[1] Valentinian I and Valens.
[2] Strictly half-brother, Gratian, whose mother was Marina Severa, the first wife of Valentinian I.

3. quodsi pares animo vires senatus habuisset, scires in publico amore perennitatis tuae esse divitias. sed maluit clementiae tuae solutionis fide placere quam magnitudine perfidae sponsionis. dehinc sub imperatore primaevo sanus muneris modus votum est saepe faciendi. absit, ut bono principi plus quam possumus ingeramus; amantium quippe largitio non iure deterit offerentes. ergo et nunc libens sume sacro aerario decreta subsidia et futuris processibus imperii tui obsequiorum similium spem reserva.

3. If the resources of the senate had been equal to its feelings for you, you would know what riches your Perennity possesses in public affection. But it preferred to please your Clemency by a faithful payment rather than by cheating you with the promise of a large sum. Henceforth, since we are ruled by a young Emperor, sensible moderation in the size of a gift is really a prayer that we may often have to make it. Far from it that we should press upon a good emperor more than we can properly manage: for, when generosity is inspired by affection, it is not right that it should wear down the donors. So too on this occasion take with pleasure for the sacred treasury[3] the subventions we have voted, and for future successful enterprises of your reign cherish the hope of similar expressions of our duty.[4]

[3] A loose term for imperial funds. The contribution went to the account of the *largitiones*, which under a *comes sacrarum largitionum* received taxes paid in gold and silver and disbursed its receipts in paying the (cash) wages of the army and civil service.

[4] The word *decennalia* seldom occurs, *CTh.* 4. 13. 1, Paneg. 3. 1, *CIL* 6. 1203, and on coins: also in S.H.A. *Gall.* 21. 5.

14

As prefect of the city in charge of all guilds (*corpora*) Symmachus had been ordered to impose a levy of horses on all *negotiatores*. He takes up their cause, pointing out that there is a limit to the burdens the *corpora* can bear: an extra imposition might well be too much. The Emperor would be well advised to give way, as his father had done years ago. Otherwise his reputation will suffer; and it is hinted that civil disturbance might follow.

D. N. VALENTINIANO SEMPER AVG.
SYMMACHVS V. C. PRAEFECTVS VRBIS

Habeant hoc publicae necessitates, ut inpossibilia plerumque persuadeant, domine imperator, sed cauto opus est, ne asperitas negotii effectu inrito solas arcessat offensas, quae nulli magis evitandae sunt, quam iuveni et principi, cuius gratia cum aetate debet adolescere. ergo numinis vestri famam simulque arduum re*i* cogitans corporatos negotiatores, membra aeternae urbis, ad equorum conlationem, quam litteris imperastis, vocare dubitavi, ne librationem clementiae vestrae querella publica praeveniret. integra res est: adhuc salubritatem consilii diligentioris expectat. iustitiae praestate, quod remittetis invidiae.

2. de exemplo veniunt, quae cavemus: siquidem caeli particeps parens clementiae vestrae, cum munus exiguum huic hominum generi mandare temptasset, motus libertate plebis abstinuit. et certe paucorum curam res illa poscebat magisque officium desiderabatur tractandae pecuniae publicae quam dispendium conferendae. consuluit tamen gloriae suae, ne quid iuberet invitis, et diligentissimus ac serius imperator speratum emolumentum tamquam popularis ignovit.

3. nec putet aeternitas vestra ab incepto temere destitisse

TO OUR LORD VALENTINIAN, FOR EVER AUGUSTUS, FROM SYMMACHUS, OF THE DISTINGUISHED ORDER OF SENATORS PREFECT OF THE CITY

I grant that public exigencies often suggest impossible measures, my Lord Emperor. But there is need of caution, lest harshness should fail to get things done and merely cause ill-feeling. No one ought to be more careful to avoid ill-feeling than a young man and an emperor; his popularity ought to increase with his years. Having in mind your Divinity's own reputation and reflecting on the difficulty of the situation I have hesitated to call upon the guild of *negotiatores*,[1] who are an essential part of the eternal city, to make a contribution of horses for the imperial needs, as indeed your dispatch ordered me to do. I do not want a public outcry to hinder the even tenor of your Clemency's reign. The matter is still open; it still awaits a sound decision more carefully thought out. Give justice the opportunities you will otherwise give to adverse criticism of yourself.

2. There is a precedent for the precautions I am taking. Your Clemency's father, who now has his membership in heaven, attempted to impose on this class of men a trifling obligation, but he was influenced by considerations of the liberty of the people and refrained.[2] Admittedly that matter made demands on the efforts of few, and the aim was to satisfy the emperor's duty to manage public finance properly rather than to cause others the expense of contributing to it. Nevertheless he had regard for his own reputation, being anxious not to impose orders on people against their will. This most careful and serious-minded Emperor denied himself a revenue he had hoped for and acted like any champion of the people.

3. Do not let your Eternity imagine that a man almost a god

---

[1] A vague term which denotes anyone who had anything to sell, goods or services.

[2] *CTh.* 14. 2. 1 (364) shows that Symmachus' father had resisted a similar levy or tax on a particular guild and that Valentinian I had withdrawn his demand and restored the old privileges of immunity. Symmachus tactfully does not refer to his father.

deo proximum virum; noverat horum corporum ministerio tantae urbis onera sustineri. hic lanati pecoris invector est, ille ad victum populi cogit armentum, hos suillae carnis tenet functio, pars urenda lavacris ligna conportat, sunt qui fabriles manus augustis operibus adcommodent, per alios fortuita arcentur incendia. iam caupones et obsequia pistoria, frugis et olei baiulos multosque id genus patriae servientes enumerare fastidium est. ad summam liquet privilegium vetus magno inpendio constare Romanis; iugi obsequio inmunitatis nomen emerunt. 4. quod si adiciantur insolita, forsitan consueta cessabunt. quare paternum clementiae tuae ingerimus exemplum. praetuli oraculum, quod pius successor imiteris. oro atque obsecro, ne populum, quem triumphantes saepe veneramini, ceteris urbibus conferatis. dabit fortuna melior, quidquid castrensis usus efflagitat; humanitatis merito necessitas vestra sedabitur.

abandoned his plan without due thought; he knew that the burdens of this great city were shouldered by the services of these guilds. One guild transports wool-bearing sheep to the city, another drives in herds to feed the people. The purveying of pork engages some, others convey wood for the furnaces of the public washing-places; there are also those who train their craftsmen's hands to make noble works; others fight fires that happen to break out. It would be tedious to give a list—innkeepers, those who serve the bake-houses, carriers of corn and oil, and the crowds of people of that kind who minister to their country.³ In short, it is clear that a long-established privilege costs Romans a good deal. By sheer services rendered they have bought immunity. 4. Now, if services to which they are unaccustomed are added, there is a risk that those to which they are already accustomed will languish. That is why we impress on you the precedent of your Clemency's father. I have put before you his pronouncement⁴ which it is for you to imitate as his dutiful successor. I beg and beseech you not to equate with all other cities the people whom in your triumphs you have often regarded with respect. Fortune will improve and will give you what the requirements of the imperial administration demand;⁵ if you show humanity, it will win you alleviation of your present needs.

³ Pork, see **22**: the supply of wood was in the care of *mancipes salinarum* (**44**) and was conveyed by *navicularii* (**44**): craftsmen, probably builders and masons. The fire-service of Augustus (*vigiles*) had disappeared by now and fire-fighting was in the hands of *centonarii*, a roll of members of the guilds who turned out in case of fire. Innkeepers catered for public servants on the move. Bakers: distribution of bread had replaced the distribution of corn: Symmachus is always anxious lest the supply should fail, cf. **18, 35**. Oil, **35**.

⁴ *CTh*. 14. 2. 1.

⁵ *Castrensis*: the imperial administration was thought of as *militia*, and posts in the civil service were designated in military terms, cf. **42**.

15

Symmachus sends New Year presents (*strenae*) to the Emperor as a symbol of loyalty from the magistrates (cf. 7). *Strenae* were by this time condemned by Christians because of their associations, so that there is a certain religious significance in this dispatch which must have been sent in December. See the additional note on p. 238.

DDD. NNN. VALENTINIANO THEODOSIO ET
ARCADIO SEMPER AVGGG. SYMMACHVS
V. C. PRAEFECTVS VRBIS

Ab exortu paene urbis Martiae strenarum usus adolevit auctore Tatio rege, qui verbenas felicis arboris ex luco Streniae anni novi auspices primus accepit, ddd. imperatores. nomen indicio est, viris strenuis haec convenire virtute atque ideo vobis huiusmodi insigne deberi, quorum divinus animus magis testimonium vigilantiae quam omen expectat. 2. sumite igitur, defensores publicae salutis, sollemniter auro ducta munuscula, non quia divitis metalli honore gaudetis, sed ut nostra devotio felicis saeculi testetur opulentiam. bonis principibus bene parta libamus. suscipite a iudicibus aperta obsequia, qui pretia occulta damnatis. merito vobis sollemnes pateras cum quinis solidis ut numinibus integritatis offerimus, quibus nec vester pudor nec noster census oneratur. 3. maneat aevum talis circa vos usus officii et honorem clementiae vestrae interminus annorum recursus instauret. libenter strenis sollemnibus praefectura fungetur strenuis deferenda.

TO OUR LORD VALENTINIAN, FOR EVER
AUGUSTUS, FROM SYMMACHUS, OF THE
DISTINGUISHED ORDER OF SENATORS
PREFECT OF THE CITY

Almost from the birth of the city of Mars the practice of giving New Year presents (*strenae*) has grown. Its originator was King Tatius who was the first to receive such presents, branches of vervain from a flourishing tree in the Grove of Strenia, to bring luck for the New Year, my Lords Emperors. The word itself shows that *strenae* corresponds to 'strenuous' men in meaning, and for that reason a mark of respect of this kind is due to you; for your divine mind looks for proof of alertness rather than a mere sign of it. 2. Take then, you protectors of the public weal, these small gifts of gold fashioned in the usual way, not because you take pleasure in the distinction of precious metal, but rather that our devotion to you may witness to the wealth of these fortunate times. And so we offer to good emperors, as though pouring a libation, what prosperity has produced: accept from the magistrates this open expression of their loyalty, you who dislike all secret payments. You have deserved that we should present the usual bowls together with five gold pieces to you who are the divinities ensuring our well-being; they will be no burden to your self-respect or to our purse. 3. May similar loyalty to you, practically demonstrated, attend your age and may the endless years as they return renew the honour paid to your Clemencies. Gladly will the prefecture discharge its accustomed duty of offering you *strenae*, for only to 'strenuous' men must it be entrusted.

16

(From this point to the end the *Relationes* have no title of addressee; some of them are headed 'DDD. NNN.').

Euphasius died and left a will in which he nominated heirs (these heirs must have been *extranei* i.e. not children or parents, for otherwise a case by some remoter member of the family would have had no chance). They applied to the praetor for leave to enter upon possession; the praetor must have satisfied himself that the will was valid and granted possession. Meanwhile some relations—*proximi*, but we are not told how close—wanted the will declared invalid. The heirs, now in possession, wanted the matter cleared up and asked for a ruling. It was explained to both parties that the procedure was for Priscianus and Polemonianus to give notice (thirty days) of their intention to bring a suit against the heirs. But they became impatient and lodged an appeal to the Emperor (before the conclusion of the case, see § 1, 'though no previous judgement had been passed'), and this was wrong, for appeal from a *praeiudicium* was forbidden. Asked their reason they said this course had been suggested to them by 'others' (who are not specified). Symmachus' department thereupon invoked a constitution which imposed a fine on litigant and judge alike if an appeal was allowed to go forward which had been made to defeat or delay the carrying out of a testator's intentions. But Symmachus feels that the *proximi* had acted on unwise advice, and did the constitution apply in such a case? (Date before 29 November, see **28.**)

DDD. NNN.

Profiteor ultro, quod scio clementiam vestram posse rescribere: verecunde potius quam iure suscepi provocationem non extante sententia, ne existimarer offensus liberae quidem sed inmaturae vocis obiectu, ddd. imppp. nam cum inter proximos Euphasii c. m. viri itemque heredes scriptos, qui olim beneficio praetoris corporibus defruuntur, super testamenti iure actio verteretur et sententiam de possessione inpatienter exigerent, quibus ab intestato bonorum possessio minime conpetebat, quia heredibus scriptis secundum tabulas docebatur indulta, Priscianus et Polemonianus ad denuntiationem dilato negotio provocarunt, (2) et cum ab *i*is ratio quaereretur, alios vocis suae incentores fuisse testati sunt, ut gesta litteris conexa monstrabunt. nec officium partibus defuit ad multam praeiudicii suggerendam, sed iudicem vestri saeculi decuit vim constitutionis[a] sacro oraculo reservare, cum allegaverint petitores, quod se ad incautam provocationem alienus hortatus inpulerit.

[a] *Seeck suggests* vindictam *for* vim, *or, alternatively, inserting* exerendam *after* constitutionis

TO OUR LORDS

I take the initiative in declaring what I know your Clemencies can reply to me: I was influenced by good feeling rather than by legal considerations when I accepted an appeal to you though no previous judgement had been passed, so that it should not be thought that I had been put out when confronted with a plea by a free but inexperienced person, my Lords Emperors. The case turned on the legality of a will; the parties were the next of kin of Euphasius, of distinguished memory, and the heirs nominated in the will, who by leave of the praetor had for some time been enjoying the assets. A ruling about possession of property was impatiently demanded by the party which, if the man died intestate, were by no means entitled to enjoy possession. Because it was shown that the nominated heirs had been granted possession according to the terms of the will, Priscianus and Polemonianus, when the business was held up with a view to their giving formal notice of prosecuting, lodged an appeal. 2. When they were asked their reason, they testified that others had incited them to make appeal, as indeed the minutes attached to the documents will show. My department did not fail in its proper role and indicated the fine attaching to a hearing out of due course;[1] but it was fitting for a magistrate of your times to reserve for your own imperial pronouncement what would amount to a 'constitution', since the petitioners stated that they had been pushed by others into an incautious appeal.[2]

[1] The department quoted a constitution, *CTh*. 11. 36. 26 (379), which inflicted a fine on the appellant and also on the judge who let the appeal through.

[2] This dispatch secured from the Emperor a relaxation of the previous rule: appeal *a praeiudicio* is allowed by a constitution addressed to Symmachus and dated 29 November 384 (*CTh*. 11. 30. 44). Thus **28** was sent before this date and **33** after.

It is clear from this dispatch, as also from **19**, that Symmachus tried cases of *querela inofficiosi testamenti*.

17

With some courage Symmachus complains that on his shoulders falls the responsibility of his office and yet his officials, whom he did not appoint, are of inferior quality. It would be better to appoint able men against their will in order to obtain better civil servants.

DDD. NNN.

Fidem meam convenit amor saeculi vestri et cura rei publicae, ne corrigenda dissimulem, ddd. imppp. cum ad praefecturam urbanam civilium rerum summa pertineat, minoribus officiis certa quaedam membra creduntur; quibus regendis industrios et probatos oportebat adhiberi, ut suum quisque munus inculpata facilitate promoveat. 2. tales nunc de iudicio numinis vestri publicus usus expectat. sed nolo culpare praesentes, cum satis sit sollicitudini meae, si melioribus viris officia intramurana mandetis. meis quippe umeris rerum omnium pondera sustinentur cedentibus reliquis, quos clementiae vestrae multiplex occupatio probare non potuit. habet temporum felicitas digniores; bonorum virorum vena fecunda est. melius urbi vestrae in posterum consuletis, si legatis invitos.

TO OUR LORDS

My love for your reign, my care for the state join my sense of loyalty in preventing me from hiding things which ought to be put right, my Lords Emperors. The highest interests of the civil administration pertain to the prefecture of the city. Certain departments of it are entrusted to minor offices;[1] to supervise them hard-working and properly proved men should have been appointed so that each employee could carry out his duties irreproachably and smoothly. 2. That is the kind of man that the public interest now expects from the good judgement of your Divinities. I do not want to blame those now occupying the posts; it satisfies my anxiety if you will give these responsibilities within the city walls to better men. For it is on my shoulders that the burden of the whole administration lies; the rest sink under it; they were men whom your Clemencies' absorption in many other matters prevented you from proving. These prosperous times possess men more worthy of the posts; indeed there is a rich vein of really good men. You will serve the interests of the city better in the future if you appoint men even against their will.

[1] Or 'officials'. Transfer of officials from one *officium* to another was limited, cf. *CTh.* 8. 4.

18

The main anxiety weighing on the *praefectus urbi* was fear of riot which might be provoked by failure of supplies of oil, grain, wood, etc. (Amm. 19. 10), or by requisitions, or by the passions aroused by the games (Amm. 14. 6. 25, 15. 7. 2), or by strife between pagans and Christians; the mob might turn against him and his property and he might suffer the anger of the Emperor. For Symmachus' anxiety cf. **6, 9, 35**.

DDD. NNN.

Felicitas quidem vestra aeternae urbi sollemnis alimoniae copiam pollicetur, ddd. imppp., sed re magis quam spe tuti esse debemus. quod facile factu est, si hanc quoque partem clementiae vestrae cura respexerit. 2. nam aestate provecta cum ex Africanis portibus minimum devehatur, non inani tangimur metu, ne res annonaria in graves cogatur angustias, et ideo oro quaesoque perennitatis vestrae salubre praesidium, ut iudices Africanos et notarium, cui aeternitas vestra mandavit frumentarios commeatus, severiora scripta destimulent, missis in hoc negotium strenuis, qui onera consueta, dum tractabilis navigatio est, victui urbis exhibeant. 3. hoc saeculo vestro, hoc divinis virtutibus dignum est, ut securitatem Romani populi inter praecipua et prima curetis. aderunt optatis cursibus plena navigia et Romanos portus frequens atque onusta classis intrabit, si adspiraverint numinis vestri secunda suffragia.

This dispatch shows that about August or September (*aestate provecta*) scarcity was causing Symmachus much alarm, and so he appealed to the Emperor for aid. A prefect could do little: he could buy corn in the provinces if available, or levy from senatorial landowners with imperial permission; both courses took time; and he could expel *peregrini*, as indeed Symmachus did on this occasion, *Ep.* 2. 7; for such expulsion cf. Amm. 14. 6. 19.

TO OUR LORDS

Your good fortune promises the Eternal City a plentiful supply of its usual maintenance, my Lords Emperors, but we ought to be made safe in fact, not in expectation. That can easily be done the moment your Clemencies' care of things has regard for this side of your administration as well as others. 2. The summer is far advanced:[1] very little has been shipped from African harbours and we experience a touch of fear, not groundless, that the corn supply has got into serious difficulties: for this reason I beg and beseech your Perennities, who are the safeguard of our welfare, that a pretty stern dispatch may prod into action the African magistrates and the *notarius* to whom your Eternities have entrusted the transportation of grain:[2] I ask you to send some energetic men to produce in visible form, while sailing is still feasible, the cargoes to which we are accustomed for the victualling of the city. 3. Your reign, your divine qualities of character, demand that one of your first and principal cares should be freedom from care for the Roman people. Ships will make the voyages we desire and will arrive full, and a numerous and heavily laden fleet will enter Roman harbours once your Divinities' favourable help wafts them along.

[1] Date of dispatch August?
[2] The *praefectus urbi* informed the praetorian prefect of Africa of the needs of the city: he in turn notified the *praefectus annonae* in Africa, who passed on orders to the *navicularii*. For *notarius* see Glossary.

19

This is an extremely difficult dispatch in which Symmachus submits a legal case for decision. It should be said in extenuation of his obscure statement of it that the relevant papers were attached. Briefly, Marciana senior pleads through her agent Liberius that her niece, Marciana junior, represented by her guardian Gaudentius, received too much of the estate of her grandmother, and too much from her father Placidianus. She therefore submits an appeal (*supplicatio*). After preliminary skirmishing the argument resolves itself into a plea (i) that Prisca had made an unfair will (*inofficiosi testamenti querela*) and (ii) that Marciana junior had received too much in gifts from her father while he was alive (*immodicarum donationum querela*). Meanwhile the time limit for valuations of the property had expired. Symmachus is at a loss.

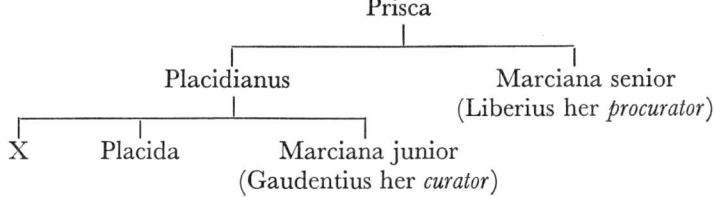

X has to be assumed because all the heirs, not two, are spoken of in the *Relatio*. But it may be that X was a daughter of Marciana senior whose interest Liberius was protecting.

See also the additional note on p. 238.

DDD. NNN.

Difficilis est exitus veterum iurgiorum; res enim multis agitata iudiciis et actionum varietate et cognoscentium motu et personarum mutationibus inplicatur, ddd. imppp. ut mihi nunc venit usus, cum inter Gaudentium curatorem Marcianae clarissimae feminae itemque Liberium procuratorem amitae eius, eodem nomine dum viveret nuncupatae, annosum luctamen audirem.

2. nam in ipso limine quaestionis, cum procuratio, quam c. m. f. senior Marciana mandaverat, invalida diceretur, quod ante cuidam Principio esset iniuncta, ubi refusas in dominam conperimus actiones atque actis praetoriis in Liberium denuo iure translatas, obiectum cassae praescriptionis amovimus.

3. tunc defensio partis adversae negavit stare personam, cuius procurationem superioris gesta iudicii non tenerent. contra neque exactam prius mandati recitationem et inter partes tributum procuratori beneficium reparationis aiebant. huic parti longius quam oportuit inmorata contentio est. sed quia prior cognitor ut iusto defensori restituerat temporum cursum, qui per actores non potest impetrari, et procuratio legebatur praetoris allegata iudicio, haec quoque praescriptio conquievit.

4. successit aliud, ut obitu Marcianae c. m. f. mandatum

TO OUR LORDS

It is difficult for long-standing disputes to find an ending. A matter treated in many courts gets into a tangle; the legal processes change, judges move, and the persons implicated are different, my Lords Emperors. I have practical experience of this at the moment; for I have listened in court to a squabble which has lasted for many years between Gaudentius, the guardian of Marciana, a woman of distinguished rank, and Liberius, her aunt's agent; she too was called Marciana while she was alive.

2. At the very outset of the case the mandate as agent which the elder Marciana, of distinguished memory, had laid upon Liberius was declared invalid on the ground that it had formerly been laid upon a certain Principius; we learnt that suits brought against the principal were refused and by orders of the praetor[1] were rightly redirected as fresh cases against Liberius; we then set aside the impediment of an objection which was null and void.

3. Thereupon the other side's attorney maintained that, since the proceedings in an earlier court contained no record of the agency, the agent had no legal standing; on the other side it was urged that the reading aloud of the deed of agency had not been demanded and that by agreement between the parties the grant of a renewal of time had been made to the agent;[2] the pleadings had caused this party a longer delay than was allowed. But, because the judge in an earlier court gave Liberius renewal of time—and it was given to him as being the recognized litigant since this right cannot be obtained by mere representatives—and because the deed of appointment was read and declared valid in the praetor's court, this objection also collapsed.

4. The next event was that Marciana, of distinguished memory,

[1] Not trying the case, but asked for his authoritative opinion.

[2] *Reparatio* (sc. *temporis*) is permission to extend a stated time (cf. **32**. 2, **39**. 3), here the time normally fixed between notice of a case and readiness to proceed. A *cognitio* began when the prosecutor brought a *denuntiatio* against the defendant in court. The case must be ready to start within four months; otherwise it lapsed. Extension could be given if the Emperor gave leave, *CTh*. 2. 6. 1, and was automatic if one of the litigants died, 2. 6. 3, *CIust*. 7. 66. 6, or if the judge fell ill, *CTh*. 11. 31. 2. In a case of *possessio* the prosecutor had to inform publicly the *possessor* that renewal had been given, 2. 6. 4.

diceretur extinctum. sed contra venerabilis Iuliani sanctio stare procuratorum iussit officia causarum dominis viventibus inchoata. ergo cum et reparationem superstite Marciana et conventionem partis adversae super aestimandis bonis Liberius impetrasset, pronuntiavimus non perisse mandatum.

5. dehinc petitore properante, ut ex constitutione numinis vestri servandi debiti causa in materna corpora mitteretur, quod adversaria aestimationem bonorum conventa facere noluisset, responsum est, de supplicationis fide prius esse tractandum. id quia probabile videbatur, admisi.

6. facto autem aditu de precibus disputandi defensor c. f. Marcianae notare sibi visus est mendacium supplicantis, quod, cum Priscae matris suae testamento neptes eius ex Placidiano genitas hereditatem cepisse dixisset, non omnes neptes ab ea scriptas probaret heredes. responsum est, de *iis* tantum, quas avia heredes instituit, supplicatum nec usquam factam omnium mentionem sed earum, quibus fuerat delata successio.

7. his deiectum curatoris patrocinium coepit exigere, ut petitor ediceret, ex quibus nominibus propositae descenderent actiones. tunc e diverso veniens ex Placidiani c. m. viri nomine, qui pater adultae fuit, inmodicarum donationum causam manasse respondit; supplementum vero unciarum ut ab herede Placidae, cui soror Marciana successit,

died and the appointment was declared terminated. But against this was the ordinance of the venerable Julian which enjoined that agents' services in lawsuits were still valid if the services had been begun in the lifetime of the principal.[3] And so, since Liberius had obtained, while Marciana was alive, both renewal of time and also agreement with the other party about the valuation of the property, we pronounced that the appointment was not extinct.

5. When the plaintiff then made hurried preparation for bringing a suit, in accordance with a constitution[4] of your Divinities, against the property of Marciana's mother with a view to safeguarding the assets as being assets owed to Marciana senior on the ground that the other party, when approached, refused to make a valuation of the property, the reply was made that before that was done there must be agreement about the accuracy of the appeal. It seemed to me that this plea was reasonable and I allowed it.

6. But, when the hearing of arguments about the appeal came on, the attorney for Marciana, a woman of distinguished rank, thought he detected a flaw introduced into the appeal by the appellant; the flaw was this—when he said that by the will of Prisca, her mother, Prisca's granddaughters, daughters of Placidianus, had taken up the inheritance, he did not prove that all the granddaughters were named by her. The reply was that the appeal concerned only those whom the grandmother had expressly described as heirs, and that there was no mention anywhere of 'all', but only of those to whom the succession had actually been given.

7. Defeated in this point the agent's attorney began to demand that the petitioner should declare on what counts the proposed suits were brought. Shifting his ground he said that a suit for 'excessive donations' derived from Placidianus, a senator now deceased—that was the count—,who was father of the girl (*Marciana junior*); he asserted that he demanded a payment to make up the loss in the same proportion as the inheritance received by the heir of Placida; her heir was in fact her sister

---

[3] *CTh.* 2. 12. 1.

[4] Not known. A *missio in possessionem* (a limited form of possession) could be ordered with a view to preserving the status of the property of, for example, bankrupts or debtors.

adseruit postulari. haec adversarius eatenus refellebat, ut diceret c. f. iuniorem Marcianam non Placidiani tantum patris successionem sed etiam Placidae germanae suae pro certis unciis consecutam, nec tamen ullam Placidae mentionem precum serie contineri.

8. sed cum allegatio diversae partis adstrueret, rem se obnoxiam persequi designatis titulis actionum et id, quod in litem venit, pro certa parte Marcianam c. f. possidere eiusque nomen cum designatione causarum doceret precibus conprehensum, stetit iudicii mei deliberatio, hoc adserente, personam Placidae supplicationi adici debuisse, illo negante, post designationem rei et eius personae, quae hodie possessione corporum defruitur, quidquam esse quaerendum.

9. accessit cunctationi meae causa vehementior, quod iubente lege, ut intra quattuor menses ad aestimationem bonorum possessor *petitori*^a teneatur, nunc, ut gesta monstrabunt, angustum nimis ex conventione tempus fuisse visum est peregrinis corporibus aestimandis.

10. et ideo motus ambiguis oraculo numinis vestri discingenda cuncta servavi; nam in rebus dubiis una salubritatis est via, ut divina quaeque vel deo proxima consulantur. coniunctae paginae allegationes partium et supplementa sumpserunt; quae cum maiestatis vestrae iustitia perpenderit, precor, ut metas curiosae liti absoluta definitione ponatis.

[a] *Mercer*: apetitore *MSS*.

Marciana.[5] This point was rebutted by his opponent in so far as he said that the younger Marciana, of distinguished rank, had obtained right of succession not only to Placidianus, her father, but also to Placida, her sister, with a specified portion of the estate and yet there was no mention of Placida in the series of petitions.

8. However, a statement by the opposite party added that he was pursuing a property which was subject to stated titles of action and that the property which came into dispute Marciana, of distinguished rank, possessed in the specified proportion; he stated too that her name together with a designation of the cases had been included in the petitions. At this point the deliberations of my court came to a halt, the one side asserting that the person of Placida ought to be added to the appeal, the other denying that, after the property had been clearly defined, as also the person at present enjoying possession, there was anything else to be demanded. 9. There was an additional, more urgent reason for my delay; the law enjoins that within a period of four months allowed for the valuation of the property the possessor shall be stayed, in the interest of the petitioner, but in the present case, as the minutes will show, the time agreed on between the parties appeared to be too short for the valuation of the property abroad.

10. Disturbed then by these perplexing problems I reserved everything for disentanglement by a pronouncement of your Divinities; where there is so much doubt there is only one way of salvation—to consult an authority which is divine or indeed next to god. The sheets gathered together here have included the declarations of the parties and the supplementary statements. When your Majesties' sense of justice has weighed them all up, I beg you to set up a finishing-post for this tedious litigation by a definite ruling.

[5] The *supplementum* was a sum making up a supposed deficiency. Liberius wants it to be assessed at the proportion of the estate Marciana junior received under her sister's will. Legacies were defined in twelfths: thus if the heir was left one-twelfth and the law said he should have received three-twelfths, he could sue for the difference to be made up (*supplementum*).

20

4 and 20 should be read together, for each supplements the other.

Gratian ordered that the Prefect of the City should make use of a *carruca* ornamented with panels of beaten or chased silver, in place of the old-fashioned *carpentum*; the cost of making this coach was to be met from imperial funds. The prefect was then Anicius Auchenius Bassus. He started to carry out the order, but found that the fisc had not the metal available; he hinted (unofficially?), so it was later thought, to the Emperors that other means of getting the metal were being tried. In spring 384 Bassus retired and Sallentius Aventius succeeded him, and then came Symmachus. He detested the idea of the *carruca*, wrote to Valentinian (4)—for Gratian had died in August 383—and asked that the order should be rescinded. Valentinian must have agreed, and he ordered that the metal should be restored to the fisc. Symmachus protested; Valentinian, he agreed, was correct in remembering that the making of a coach was to be at the expense of imperial funds, but he had forgotten the 'intimation' of Bassus; Symmachus had caused (under imperial orders?) an inquiry to be made and found that the silver had been provided by various chests not controlled by the Emperor, and also by private individuals. But he also found that the fisc, acting on Valentinian's ruling, had seized the silver. Naturally the contributors wanted their silver to be returned to them since now the coach was not to be built: would the Emperor please instruct the *largitionum sacrarum comes* to restore the silver to its rightful owners?

DDD. NNN.

Cum clementia vestra meminisset faciendae carrucae inpendium de sacro aerario esse decretum, censuit, ut eius argentum publicis conditis redderetur, ddd. imppp. sed examinis repperit fides ex aliis titulis adsumptam speciem, quam vehiculi ornatus accepit. cuius rei etiam vir inlustris prodecessor meus Auchenius Bassus perennitati vestrae rationem dicitur intimasse; et ideo saeculi vestri aequitas imperavit, ut examinata et conperta suggererem.

2. cum fiscus in tempore, quod praebendum fuerat, non haberet, ex arca quaestoria itemque ex formarum conditis, praeterea ex argentariorum parsimonia argentum iusso operi ministratum est, cuius solutio, si carrucae usus maneret, de thesauris imperialibus iure peteretur. 3. sed nunc carpenti novitate submota suum quisque deposcit, nec difficile credimus impetrari, quod a legum parentibus postulatur. quaeso, ut digna temporibus responsa reddatis, quo v. c. et inlustris sacrarum largitionum comes refundendum esse cognoscat publicis titulis privatisque personis, quod sine lacuna imperialis aerarii deprompsit aliena conlatio.

TO OUR LORDS

Since your Clemencies remembered that the cost of making the coach was to be met, it was decided, by the sacred imperial treasury, you ruled that the silver should be returned to the public funds, my Lords Emperors. But a very faithful examination has discovered that the material which was used in the decoration of the conveyance was derived from other accounts. An *illustris*, Auchenius Bassus,[1] the last-but-one occupant of my office, is said to have acquainted your Perennities with the reason; and therefore the justice of your reign has instructed me to make an investigation and report my findings to you.

2. The imperial fisc did not possess at the time the silver it was required to furnish, and so for the purposes of the work which had been commanded it was supplied by the quaestors' chest,[2] by the reserves in the aqueduct account,[3] and by the self-denial of private silversmiths; and, if the proposal to use a coach of this description had been maintained, payment for the silver would rightly have been claimed from the local imperial depots.[4]

3. But now the new look to be given to the wagon has been cancelled, and everyone is demanding back his own; we do not think it would be difficult for the authors of our laws to grant what is asked of them. I beg you to send a reply worthy of the times so that the *sacrarum largitionum comes*, of the distinguished order of senators and an *illustris*, may know that he must refund to public accounts and to private individuals all the silver which the voluntary contributions from other sources made available, thereby saving the imperial treasury from depleting its assets.

[1] Anicius Auchenius Bassus, proconsul of Campania; *praefectus urbi* 22 November 382 to 383 and perhaps the first few weeks of 384; a Christian, so too his wife Tyrrhenia. For his career see Dess. 1262, 1292, 5702, 8984. His daughter married Olybrius.

[2] The senatorial treasury, also known as *arca publica*.

[3] *Forma* was the mould from which the conduits of the aqueducts were made (Front. *Aq.* 75, *Dig.* 7. 7. 27. 3). It was used also of the aqueduct itself (Front. *Aq.* 126).

[4] A *thesaurus* was a local store with offices attached which kept supplies of goods owned by the government, cf. e.g. *CTh.* 8. 7. 14; they were spread all over the Empire and were under the general supervision of a *comes thesaurorum*.

21

The circumstances of this letter have to be inferred from the letter itself, for we do not possess the vital constitution, only a reference to it. The date is probably November; Praetextatus and Damasus are alive, but the opposition to Symmachus is great.

In 382 Symmachus had led a deputation to Gratian at Milan asking that the Altar of Victory might be restored (see **3**). Gratian refused even to see the deputation (**3.** 1), for a counter-petition had been drawn up by Christian senators and forwarded to Damasus, Bishop of Rome, who sent it to Ambrose to be forwarded to the Emperor. They said they would absent themselves from meetings of the senate (Ambrose, *Ep.* 17. 10). In 383 Gratian died and harvests were bad (**3.** 15); the pagan party regarded these events as due to their gods. Moreover, Praetextatus was appointed *praefectus praetorio* and Symmachus *praefectus urbi*. The party seemed to be in a stronger position and Praetextatus obtained from Valentinian, in the spring of 354, a *decretum* which set on foot an inquiry into the removal of ornaments from public places (which included temples) for private use and ordered their restoration; proceedings too were to be taken against the plunderers of the temples. (This success emboldened the party to send **3**.) The terms of the *decretum* have to be inferred from **21**, for the text is unknown.

The events which followed must again be inferred. Reports reached the Emperor that Symmachus was avenging himself by using the inquiry to maltreat Christians (§ 1). Valentinian publicly reprimanded Symmachus (§§ 2, 3), and ordered that all whom he had imprisoned should be released (§ 6). Moreover he modified his decree (§ 6). To all this Symmachus had a perfect reply: (*a*) Damasus, Bishop of Rome, testified that no harm had been done to Christians (§ 3); (*b*) the inquiry had not even started (§ 5). Symmachus felt isolated amid growing hostility; he offered his resignation, see also **10.** 2.

Scio quidem naturae humanae vitio probitatem subiacere livori, sed miror eo progressas insidias aemulorum, ut crudo mendacio insontis fama peteretur, ddd. imppp. quid enim non audeant quidve intemptatum relinquant, qui in arce terrarum Christianae legis iniuriis vindicata fana finxerunt? 2. flevit, credo, scaenae istius fabricator, cum de ecclesiae penetralibus raptos ad tormenta simularet, cum de longinquis ac finitimis urbibus duci antistites in vincla describeret; neque enim serenum clementiae tuae animum sine his argutiis conpulisset sacro edicto populum convenire, ut asperioribus, quam pietati tuae mos est, litteris praefectum, quem sine ambitu legistis, argueres. 3. reddat nunc, quisquis ille est, causas fallaciae suae, qui sub occasione iustae inquisitionis, qua me cultum spoliatorum moenium investigare iussistis, tragicas quaestiones de ministris catholicae iactavit agitatas; respondeat litteris episcopi Damasi, quibus adsectatores eiusdem religionis negavit ullam contumeliam pertulisse. non magnopere officii mei praetendo responsa,

I know that by a defect of human nature integrity can be overpowered by rancour; still, I am surprised that the secret plots of rivals can go so far as to attack with a sheer lie the reputation of an innocent man, my Lords Emperors. There is nothing they would not dare, nothing they would leave untried—these people who have made up the story that in the citadel of the world the cause of the temples has been championed by doing injury to the Christian faith.[1] 2. He shed tears, I should imagine, the inventor of that kind of drama, when he pretended that men had been dragged to the torture-chamber from the sanctuaries of the church, when he described how from distant and neighbouring cities priests had been haled off to prison. For without trickery of this kind he would never have prevailed on your Clemencies' calmness of mind to address the people by imperial edict,[2] in order that you might arraign in a dispatch expressed in harsher terms than is your Pieties' custom a prefect whom, though he never sought the post, you did in fact choose. 3. Let him explain the reasons for his deceit—whoever he is who, on the threshold of that justifiable inquiry which you instructed me to hold to trace the ornaments taken from the plundered strongholds (*of the temples*), spread it abroad that a heart-rending inquisition of the servants of the Catholic Church had been set on foot. Let him give his reply to the letter of Bishop Damasus[3] in which he denied that the followers of that religion had ever suffered any insulting treatment. I do not greatly shield myself behind the replies my office gave; from it an exact record of facts has been demanded precisely in order that nothing done should

[1] *Christiana lex*. For *lex* in this sense see *CTh*. 16. 5. 1 (376), Amm. 15. 7. 6. The δόγματα of Epicurus had been translated as *lex* by Cicero (*Tusc*. 5. 108): δόγμα was also used in the official sense of 'decree' (e.g. Dem. 5. 19) and in Roman times especially for *senatus consultum*. The δόγματα of Eph. 2 : 15 was interpreted by early expositors as 'the faith'.
[2] The imperial edict cannot be *CTh*. 1. 6. 9 if that is correctly dated 29 December 384, since Praetextatus and Damasus are referred to as alive. It must be assumed that Symmachus was twice reprimanded and that we have no record of the reprimand implied in this *Relatio*.
[3] Damasus, Bishop of Rome; died at the end of 384.

a quo ideo quaesita est rerum fides, ne factum aliquod recordationem cognitoris effugeret: credatur eius legis antistiti, quae laesa simulatur, credatur populo Romano, qui perennitatis vestrae admonitus edicto miratur in procinctu creditum, quod Roma nescit admissum. 4. omitto iniuriam praefecturae et conscientiae meae, quando eo processit insimulatio, ut vos quoque ipsos auctores honoris mei quadam reprehensione praestringat. nam qui summi loci iudices decolorant, sacri testimonii facilitatem videntur incessere. iam dudum me divus genitor numinis tui praecipuo honore dignatus est, ille meritorum arbiter singularis, cuius imperium cum moribus recepisti. paternum sequere, tuum tuere iudicium: qui praefecturam sine ambitu meruimus, sine offensione ponamus.

5. suggestionibus viri excellentis et de re publica bene meriti Praetextati praefecti praetorio abusus existimor. quid, si ex illo decreto, quod probabiliter impetravit, necdum a me quaestio ulla temptata est? praevidi enim, quid possint aemuli suspicari, atque ideo obsignata officio praefecturae sacra iussa commiseram. nec me huiusmodi coniectura decepit: siquidem severe executus insimulor, quod non convincor adgressus. 6. haec omnia fide actorum conprehensa subieci, unum illud adiciens, ut me perennitas vestra necessitate inquisitionis huius absolvat, cuius auctoritatem referri ad scrinia palatina iussistis. nam si tantum de me inprobis licuit extante praecepto, quid retractatis litteris non licebit? sane laudabili viro episcopo denegante ullum e suis aut carcere aut vinculis adtineri et officio eadem suggerente ignoro,

escape the investigator's notebook. No! let the priest of the faith which it is alleged has been violated be believed; let the Roman people be believed which, though admonished by your Perennities' edict, is amazed that the court circle should accept as true reports of acts of which Rome herself has no knowledge. 4. I say nothing about the wrong done to the office of prefect, or to my sense of honour, when false accusation is carried to such lengths that criticism smears you too as having put me into this high office. For people who denigrate high-ranking magistrates give the impression of attacking the Emperor's judgement of a man as being too casual. In the past your Divinity's late father honoured me with a chief office:[4] he was a remarkable judge of merit and you have taken over his empire and his character. Follow your father's judgement, preserve your own; and let me, who was thought worthy of the prefecture though I never sought it, lay it down without causing you offence.

5. I am thought to have gone too far in carrying out the proposals of the excellent Praetextatus, a great public servant and prefect of the praetorian guard.[5] And what happens to this charge if as a matter of fact I have not yet acted on the decree he very laudably obtained (*from the Emperor*) and have not yet started any investigation? You see, I foresaw the suspicions my rivals could harbour and for that reason I had already committed the imperial instructions to the keeping of the prefecture's office under seal. A guess like that did not let me down; for I am now attacked for being harsh in carrying through measures which I am not proved even to have started. 6. All this I have appended in a faithfully accurate minute, adding the request that your Perennities should release me from the need to carry out this investigation, the authority for which you ordered to be entered in the palatine records. For, if unscrupulous people had licence to treat me in this way while the instruction was still valid, what licence will they not have if the text of it is modified?[6] The estimable bishop denied firmly that any of his flock had been detained in prison or had been chained, and my department gave information to the same effect; I am at a loss therefore to know

---

[4] Valentinian I appointed Symmachus proconsul of Africa, 373/4.

[5] See above, 10 n. 1.

[6] *Praecepto* is taken to mean the instruction granted to Praetextatus and *litteris* to mean the text of that same *praeceptum*.

quos potissimum praeceperitis absolvi. tenent quidem leges variorum criminum reos, sed ut conperi, a ministerio Christianae legis alienos.

7. quid igitur aeternitas vestra decernat, devotus opperior et quaeso, ut fallaciam retundatis, quae divini pectoris tui sollicitavit quietem, quae ad edicti necessitatem venerandi principis curam coegit. me munivit invidia: apud aures enim sacras locum postea non habebit convicta mendacii. si quid tamen denuo obtrectantium murmur ingesserit, opto iudicium: experientur me sub imperiali disceptatione constantem, qui nocentem probare non possunt.

precisely what men you direct should be set free. It is true that men convicted of various crimes are legally held, but, as I have ascertained, none connected with the service of the Christian faith.

7. In all devotion I await your Eternities' decision and I ask that you should rebut these lying charges which have disturbed your divine peace of mind, which have engaged the attention of a most respected emperor, and have compelled him to issue this edict. Malicious rumours have in fact protected me; for henceforth when they come to the ears of the Emperors they will find no abiding-place, since they will have been convicted of falsehood. If, however, the murmurs of my slanderers should insinuate something else against me, then I wish for trial; those who cannot prove me guilty will find me stout-hearted if I am to be the subject of an imperial decision.

22

This dispatch places on the Emperor the onus of resolving the dilemma he has created by making his own appointment to a post in the civil service. How is it to be reconciled with existing rules of tenure and promotion? For a similar case see 27.

De tribunatu suarii fori nuper orta contentio causam mihi adtulit legum arbitros consulendi, ddd. imppp. provectus instabat, ut delatum sibi sortiretur officium; vetus e lege,[a] quae tempora istiusmodi actibus certa decrevit, recusabat honore decedere. secutus morem longa aetate servatum eum, qui recens maiestatis vestrae beneficium praeferebat, admisi; sed ut deinceps, si forte usus tulerit, cunctationem iudicii absoluta forma submoveat, statui sacrum numinis vestri oraculum sciscitari, utrum fas sit novos tribunos servata lege differri an magis veteres oporteat praelata devotione removere.

[a] *Lectius*: eligit *MSS*.

A dispute has lately arisen over the office of *tribunus suarii fori* and has made me consult you, my Lords Emperors. The holder when promoted insisted that he should obtain the office conferred on him; he is now old, and, relying on the law which has fixed definite times for these posts, he kept refusing to resign it. I followed a custom which has been observed for a long time and I admitted a man who displayed your Majesties' grant of favour. But, so that in the future, if necessity arose, a clear-cut formula might get rid of the delay caused by a judicial decision, I decided to get a pronouncement from your Divinities on this question: is it right to keep the law[1] and to let new appointments as tribune be deferred or rather to give precedence to my loyalty to you and remove old occupants of the post?

[1] Not known.

23

It is impossible to consider here the implications of this important but difficult *Relatio* in which Symmachus voices, with great justification, the grievances which he feels. Briefly, his authority is undermined by (i) a permanent department with firmly entrenched interests and powers, often acting independently of him, of which he is the nominal and temporary head, (ii) the intrigues of rival officials who are the agents of the imperial government with their own courts and executive staff, (iii) his lack of means to enforce his own decisions. The weakness of his authority encourages disloyalty in other directions, as displayed for example by a barrister of his own court. In addition to these grievances is the fear of offending the Emperor by criticizing his officials, though he does not directly express this fear; indeed the writing of this dispatch demanded not a little courage.

The dispatch falls into three related parts:

(i) suspicion of the malpractices of the *censuales*: this suspicion sparked off an inquiry into the administration of Anicius Auchenius Bassus who was Symmachus' predecessor but one as prefect of the city (§§ 1, 2).

(ii) the machinations of Ragonius Vincentius Celsus, a barrister in Symmachus' court, who had been a *socius* of one of the senators involved in (i); he revenged himself by causing trouble between Symmachus and the Vicar of Rome (§ 3; for his later career see n. 5).

(iii) the clue to the remainder of the *Relatio* is the anxiety of the *officium urbanum* to remove from the scene a certain Memorius who had contracted debts in Africa and was supposed to possess evidence against Bassus' administration. This anxiety was countered by the efforts, including violence, of imperial agents (the Vicar and Fulgentius and his own agent Felix). Symmachus does his best to assert the authority of his own department and to exercise control, but he is thwarted at every turn. Date of dispatch probably October or November.

The inquiry was reopened in 385 and it was established that

one of the *primates* of the *officium urbanum* was chiefly responsible for irregularities in the accounts of the *arca frumentaria* and *arca olearia*. Several of the *primates* were sentenced to death; Bassus was given monetary compensation, but his reputation suffered since he was in charge of the department. *CTh.* 12. 11. 2.

Vnum levamen iniuriis meis tribuit eventus, ddd. imppp., ut Romam publicae utilitatis gratia v. c. et inlustris clementiaeque vestrae semper dicatus comes Hesperius mitteretur; nam si eum testem contumeliarum, quas pertuli, non haberem, quis dubitaret, eam praefecturam, quae Romae est superior ceteris, turbidum aliquid pro potestate fecisse? is, quoniam semper amicus est veritati et famam bonorum temporum colit, si dederit aeternitas vestra copiam, contemptum legum ac saeculi non silebit: ego, ut potero, de multis pauca narrabo repetitis paululum causis, quae mihi, ut arbitror, has insidias excitarunt.

2. cum pro diligentia, quae debet omnibus inesse iudicibus, argenti publici ratio quaereretur, quod censualium editores munerum contulerunt, inter ceteras fraudes repertum est, quosdam functionibus absolutos sumptum debitum rei publicae non dedisse et, ut fallacia ista tegeretur, ex alieno argento tantundem censualibus falsis titulis inputat*um*, quantum duo conferre debuerant. hoc cum clarissimi viri sponte sine adiectione dispendii reddidissent, senatum prisco more consului, quid in communi causa patrum

A recent event has contributed one element of comfort in the wrongs which I am suffering, my Lords Emperors; to the great advantage of the state *comes* Hesperius,[1] a member of the senatorial order and an *illustris* who is ever devoted to your Clemencies, has been sent to Rome.[2] If I did not now have him to bear witness to the insults I have endured, no one would doubt that this prefecture of mine, which is superior to all the others in Rome, had created turbulence rather than exercised authority. Hesperius, being always the friend of truth and anxious to promote the good name of this good era, will not keep silence about the contempt shown for the law and the times, if your Eternities will give him the chance to speak. For myself, I will give a brief account, as far as I can, of the many things that have happened, going back a short distance into the causes which, in my opinion, have given rise to the veiled attacks on me.

2. To satisfy that attention to detail which should be a part of every magistrate, an audit was being held of the money accruing to the state from the contributions of men who had nominally provided the games actually organized by the census office. Among various other frauds it was discovered that certain people exempted from personal service had not contributed the cost of the games which was due to the state.[3] Moreover, to hide their deceit, as much had been appropriated from other funds as the two men ought to have paid, and had been credited to them by false entries in the lists. These people, of the distinguished order of senators, then voluntarily paid what was due without being called on to make any further payment;[4] therefore I followed ancient precedent and consulted the senate to see what their authority intimated in a matter which affected them all. Several

---

[1] Hesperius, perhaps the grandson of Ausonius and the son of Hesperius, *praefectus praetorio* in 377.

[2] He may have been on a routine visit or been sent to inquire into Symmachus' troubles.

[3] Senators were required to provide games: those resident away from Rome could leave it to the *censuales* to organize games on their behalf: they paid a stated sum.

[4] i.e. a fine.

SYMMACHI RELATIONES 23

innueret auctoritas. dictis aliquot sententiis factum meum reverendi ordinis probavit adsensio.

3. interiectis diebus cum Romam v. c. et laudabilis vicarius commeasset, v. c. causidicus fori mei Celsus, socius eius, qui debitum refudit inpendium, tuitionem contra me et annonae praefectum clarissimum virum de sede vicaria postulavit, cum *ego* aditus in causa publica civilem conventionem matri eius, *quae retinere adseritur patrimonium candidati,*[a] super nepotis sui munere detulissem responsione servata, praefectus vero annonae v. c. pistorem publicae annonae verbo tantum reposcere diceretur, quem manibus officialium Celsus eruerat. hic iam vestrae perennitatis est aestimare contumeliam praefecturae, cuius causidicus nihil passus auxilium secundis iudiciis impetravit.

4. *parva* haec visa sunt: quoniam patientiam meam minime perculerunt, adiectum est, quod dissimulare non possem. nam cum ad examinandos actus v. c. Bassi ex praefecto urbi potestas vicaria ad secretarium commune prodiisset, nescio quis, ut aiunt libello dato, de officii mei conludio vel iniquitate conquestus est, quod Memorius litigator iussus a Basso solvendi debiti gratia ad iudicia Africana deduci, cum et a viro inlustri decessore meo Aventio et a me

[a] *transposed by Seeck: after* servata *MSS.*

men expressed their opinion and the venerable order agreed to approve my action.

3. After a few days the Vicar, of the distinguished order of senators and highly to be commended, visited Rome. Then Celsus,[5] of the distinguished order of senators and a barrister in my court, who was associated with the man who repaid the amount owing (*for the games*), asked the Vicar's Bench to grant him protection against me and against the *praefectus annonae*, of the distinguished order of senators. I, he said, when approached in an action brought by the state, had caused an indictment (with right of reply reserved) to be entered against his mother, who is alleged to be withholding the patrimony of a *candidatus*, in the matter of the state-service of her grandson; the *praefectus annonae*, of the distinguished order of senators, was alleged to be demanding back, only by word of mouth, a baker employed by the *annona* whom Celsus had forcibly taken from the custody of officials. At this point, it is for your Perennities to assess the contempt done to the office of Prefect; a barrister of his court, who had been wronged in no way, actually asked and obtained aid in a second court.

4. These matters seemed of small account; but, since they did not in the least upset my patience, something more was done, so serious that I could not pretend it had not happened. Members of the Vicar's staff proceeded to the 'common court'[6] for the purpose of reviewing the public acts of the former prefect of the city, Bassus,[7] of the distinguished order of senators. Thereupon, some unknown person lodged a written statement (so it is said), and made formal complaint about collusion and malpractice in my department. The story was this:

Memorius, a party in a lawsuit, was ordered by Bassus to be remanded to the African courts with a view to paying his debts;

---

[5] Ragonius Vincentius Celsus, advocate in Symmachus' court; appointed (very soon after the writing of **23**) as *praefectus annonae*, which post he held for nearly four years. He won a great reputation at Ostia and Portus, see the tribute of the *mensores* and *caudicarii* in Dess. 1272, also *CIL* 6. 1760, 14. 4717–18.

[6] The court, shared by the prefect and the Vicar, known as the *urbana sedes* or *Tellurense secretarium*, on the lowest slope of the Esquiline between the *templum Telluris* and the Baths of Trajan. Dess. 5523. For the prefect and Vicar sitting together see §§ 13 and **26**. 3.

[7] See above, **20** n. 1. He had been accused of misconduct of the *arcae frumentaria* and *olearia*.

per libellos, ne eo pergeret, postulasset, navi esset abductus. hunc ilico v. c. et laudabilis vicarius, ut subscriptio libelli indicat, adesse praecepit. 5. ubi pariter ambo consedimus et seriem querellarum recitatione cognovi, admonui, ut is, qui adierat vicariam sedem, probaturus intraret. tunc officium eius hominem deesse respondit, *q*uem praecepto iudicis sui in examen accir*e* debuerat. quid hic aestimandum sit, relinquo sapientibus.

semel atque iterum praeconis vocibus advocatur nec tamen inclamatus adcurrit. 6. tunc nullo adsistente apparitio urbana coepit urgueri, quod ad Africam transvectus esset, qui Bassum clarissimum virum criminis posset arguere. suggestum est, paritum esse sententiae, quam cum Bassus post luctamen partium protulisset, provocatio non removit. ad haec Fulgentius v. c. tribunus et notarius conventos adiutores urbanae sedis adseruit, ne Memorius navigaret. a quo cum requireretur, an ad eum aliquid super Bassi criminibus Memorius detulisset, ait querellas eius libellorum paginis contineri, credo, simulare non ausus, quod accusator esse voluisset.

7. ad hoc urbani adiutor officii per Felicem sibi a clarissimo viro Fulgentio mandatum esse respondit, ut secundum sententiam Memorius ad Africam duceretur. mox Felicem censuimus adtinendum, quo posset liquere, an huius

though he had petitioned in writing both my illustrious predecessor Aventius[8] and also myself, pleading that he should not go there, he was taken off by ship. Immediately the Vicar, of the distinguished order of senators and highly to be commended, ruled that he should put in an appearance, as indeed the endorsement of the document shows. 5. Both of us took our seats together and I heard a series of complaints read in court. I gave a warning that the man who had approached the Vicar's Bench should put in an appearance to prove his points. Then an official of the Bench replied that the man was not forthcoming, the very man whom by the ruling of his own magistrate the official ought to have summoned for examination. What assessment of the situation ought to be made at this point I leave to experts.

Time after time the crier[9] summoned him, but, in spite of being cried, he did not come forward. 6. Then, since no one appeared, the lower officials of the city department began to come under fire, it being alleged that the man who could convict Bassus of offences had been carried off to Africa. It was then submitted that the terms of the sentence had simply been obeyed; since Bassus had pronounced it after the dispute of the parties, the appeal (*to Aventius and himself*) did not set it aside. On top of all this Fulgentius, of the distinguished order of senators, *tribunus et notarius*, asserted that *adiutores* of the city Bench had been approached with a view to preventing Memorius from sailing. When he was asked whether Memorius had conveyed to him anything bearing on the charges against Bassus, he said that the complaints were contained in the pages of the documents; I suppose he did not dare to pretend that he had wanted to be the accuser in the case.

7. Added to this, an *adiutor* in the city department said in reply to a question that an order had been given to him by Fulgentius, of the distinguished order of senators, that the sentence should be carried out and Memorius be taken to Africa; this order, he said, was given through the agency of Felix. We soon decided that Felix should be detained so that it might become clear whether

---

[8] Sallustius Aventius, *praefectus urbi* probably 383 to 11 June 384, immediate predecessor to Symmachus; probably identical with the Sallustius of *Ep.* 5. 55–7; lived in Spain; a pagan.
[9] The *praecones* and *nomenclatores* (§ 8) were probably the same; besides fulfilling duties in court they were also an escort to the prefect.

SYMMACHI RELATIONES 23

mandati internuntius extitisset. interea vir laudabilis vicarius, cum adessent alii, quos in Bassi causis possemus audire, ob eius absentiam, quem facile est ex Africanis revocare provinciis, iudicium omne deseruit, nescio an ex usu eorum, qui ut audirentur adfluxerant. promissa relatione discedo.

8. Felix, qui in communi iudicio iussus est adtineri, officii executione corripitur. is cum a me insequenti *die* tuitionis auxilium poposcisset et unius nomenclatoris, ut in urbe pacata, adminiculo fretus incederet post vehiculum praefecturae, iussu Fulgentii c. v. per Gaudentium et Victorem agentes in rebus et Bonifatium palatinum, qui hactenus in officio urbano militavit, violenter adreptus deducitur in eius aedes, de cuius mandatis fuerat audiendus. 9. quod cum sibi Fulgentius v. c. auctor contumeliae meae invidiosum putaret, ad circi secretarium convolavit facti inliciti volens praestare rationem, quod sibi metum fuisse dicebat, ne officii subornaretur inpulsu.

expectatis, credo, augustissimi principes, ut praefectus et iudicii vestri securus et innocentiae suae, aliquid severum censuisse dicatur: fateor, neque paenitet, animum temperavi, dum certam de vobis spero vindictam. 10. statui, ut Felix vadibus, qui Fulgentio non essent cogniti, traderetur. quid mitius decerni, quid remissius potuit? tunc ille tamquam cessurus egreditur; sed cum ad eius aedes semel atque iterum princeps officii commeasset et obstinatam hominis contumaciam non posset inflectere, inanem syngrapham reportavit, qua redhibitionem Felicis in alterum diem sponsione distulerat. tenet domi testem, quem de se noverat

there really had been an intermediary transmitting this order. Meantime the Vicar, highly to be commended, just because a man who could easily be summoned back from Africa was not in court, gave up trying any cases, though there were others present whom he could hear on the counts against Bassus. Perhaps he had had experience of the people who had flocked in to obtain a hearing. I promised the matter would be referred, and I left.

8. Felix, who had been ordered to be detained in the 'common court', was now apprehended under official instruction. On the following day he begged me for the aid of 'protection' of the court; and, assuming that the city was peaceful, he relied on only one crier to call his name as he walked behind the prefect's carriage.[10] He was forcibly seized by the orders of Fulgentius, of the distinguished order of senators, acting through Gaudentius and Victor, both *agentes in rebus*, and Bonifatius, a Palatine, who was doing state-service in the city department. He was then carried off to the house of the very man about whose orders he had been going to be questioned in court. 9. Now, since Fulgentius, of the distinguished order of senators, who was responsible for this insult to me, thought it would bring discredit on himself, he fled to the 'circus' court,[11] wishing to explain his illegal act by saying that he was afraid of having undue pressure put on him at the instigation of my department.

You are waiting, most august Emperors, for it to be said that your prefect, confident of your judgement and his own innocence, now took a stern decision. I admit—and I do not regret it—that I exercised great moderation, hoping that you would be sure to come to my defence. 10. I decided that Felix should be handed over to sureties who were not to be known to Fulgentius. I could not have taken a more gentle or a more indulgent decision. Thereupon he (*Fulgentius*) left the court, as though he was going to yield. The *princeps* of my department called at his house time after time and found it impossible to bend his stubborn arrogance; he brought back with him a worthless promissory note in which he put off restoring Felix for another day and gave a guarantee to this effect. He kept at his house the witness who, as he knew,

---

[10] See 4.
[11] A court at the Circus Maximus, attended by the prefect when he went on circuit.

audiendum; etiam huius iniuriae adsumo patientiam. culpate, ut vultis, ut dignum est: scivi meliorem esse iudicum causam, quae rerum dominis reservatur.

11. expectamus, ut altero die quam*vis* instructus officio redderetur; at ille crastina luce, ut gesta monstrabunt, adversum cautionis fidem vicariae potestati tradendus abducitur. hoc ubi princeps officii conperit, paucis comitatus excurrit; retinet Felicem celebri urbis loco nec tamen eripit; ita Fulgentius, qui se simulat verberatum, manu validiore legibus repugnavit. interea Felix a militibus vicariae potestatis abducitur, et †cum princeps officii mei sub conspectu Romanae plebis auditur.[b] videro, quid de hoc facto perennitas vestra debeat iudicare; ego ordinem tenebo gestorum. 12. fatetur sub alterius cognitoris examine litigator, nihil sibi ab apparitoribus meis adversum Fulgentium esse mandatum. hi*n*c iussu eius ad commune secretarium, quo faciendae oblationis gratia summates quosque conduxeram, a principibus officii utriusque perducitur; nihil enim repertum fuerat, quod praefecturam posset involvere.

13. tunc Fulgentius facti sui conscientia percitus, caesum se esse conqueritur; sed mox eiusdem Felicis ac devotissimi viri principis responsione pars ista purgata est. et tamen querellae eius audientiam non negavi, clarissimo et spectabili viro vicario in societatem cognitionis, si vellet, adscito . . . .[c] stuere nomina testium plebeiorum danda promisit, credo, ut per moram vel meus dolor *praeter*[d] satisfactionem mitesceret vel ipse rursus alias moliretur insidias. 14. qui,

[b] et vi princeps . . plebis avellitur *Seeck* [c] *Seeck makes no suggestion*
[d] *Suse*: om. *MSS.*

had to be heard in court giving evidence about himself. I mustered the patience to bear even this wrong. Blame me, according to your wishes, according to my deserts; I knew that magistrates have a better case if it is reserved for the judgement of the masters of the world.

11. We waited for him to be returned, however well coached as to what he was to say, to my department on the next day. But at dawn, as the minutes will show, he was haled away to be handed over to the authority of the Vicar—this in spite of the guarantee Fulgentius had given. The moment the *princeps* of my department heard of this, he rushed out with only a small escort; he laid a hand on Felix in a crowded part of the city but did not drag him out of the crowd. And so Fulgentius, who pretended that he had been struck repeatedly, resisted legal authority just because he had a stronger body of men with him. Meanwhile Felix was carried off by servicemen under the Vicar's command, and the head of my department [was forcibly torn away from Felix] in full view of the Roman people. I shall soon see what judgement your Perennities will think it their duty to give on this action; meantime I will keep to the order of the minutes.

12. The litigant Memorius examined by a second judge admitted that no orders had been given to him by my officials to do anything in respect of Fulgentius. By command of the judge he was taken away by the *principes* of both departments to the 'common court' whither I had conducted all the leading senators to make the present (*of gold to the emperor*);[12] for nothing had been discovered which could possibly involve the department of the prefect of the city.

13. Then Fulgentius, smitten with a realization of what he had done, complained that he had been beaten; very quickly that part of the proceedings was cleared up thanks to the answers of Felix and my most conscientious *princeps*. All the same I did not refuse to hear his complaints and called in the Vicar, of the distinguished order of senators and a *spectabilis*, to share the inquiry if he wished. [Fulgentius] promised [. . . to furnish] the names of some plebeian[13] witnesses; this, I imagine, was to give time for my indignation to subside (there was no question of making amends), and for new efforts at intrigue on his part. 14. As events

[12] See 13. [13] ? of no great standing and reliability.

ut res indicat, conscientia hominis subornati, a quo vicariae potestati libellus oblatus est, domestice confectis apud eundem actis ausus est postulare, ne apparitores eius, quos ob discessum litigatoris custodia carceris iusserat adtineri, iniuriae subiacerent. post haec usurpato cursu publico neglectoque iudicio audacis facti conscius evolavit, ut praefecturae iustas querimonias praeveniret, ignarus, ut res est, parentes generis humani magis iustitia quam invidia commoveri.

15. haec ita esse gesta nec ulla arte fu*c*ari, instructio subiecta testabitur. in qua repperiet aeternitas vestra, praefecturam, quam in me puro iudicio contulistis, nihil saltem ad vindictam publicae disciplinae esse molitam, cum omnibus iniuriis cederetur, quas boni quique praesumunt pro vigore saeculi vindicandas. haec enim spes et fiducia ius creditae mihi potestatis infregit, ut auctores honoris mei et publicae dignitatis et iudicii sui contumeliam iusta severitate defendant. ss. IIII. kl. Aug. Aeliano o̅c̅a̅b̅.

show, he then took into league the man who had filed the written statement with the Vicar's department and suborned him; together they privately made up a story about what had happened and he had the face to demand that his officials, whom he had ordered to be detained in the safe-keeping of a prison on account of the departure of the original defendant (*Memorius*), should not be subjected to ill-treatment. After that he took advantage of the public system of transport, absented himself from the courts, and took to flight to anticipate the justifiable complaints of the prefect's department; he was aware of the audacity of what he had done, but he did not realize that, as things are, the parents of the human race are influenced rather by their sense of justice than by malicious reports.

15. That these events took place just as I have described without any skilful embellishment, the attached document which sets them out in order will show. In it your Eternities will find that your prefect—and you bestowed the office on me on your own uninfluenced judgement—did not even make any effort to assert discipline in the public services; for we gave way before every injury offered us—injuries which every right-minded man feels should be punished if the times are to remain vigorous. Confident expectation, you see, that those who conferred my office on me should use just and stern measures to protect the dignity of the state and their own choice of prefect against insult has really impaired the authority of the powers you entrusted to me.[14]

[14] The subscription is not given in Juretus or Pareus. Meyer thinks *ss*. stands for *scripta sunt*, and an official put his name alongside the prefect's name and it has been preserved. Mr. C. H. Roberts suggests that the *o* in *ocab* might be due to dittography of the last letter of *Aeliano*, and that *cab* stands for *caballari*, horseman, dispatch-rider (*caballaris* occurs in *CIL* 8. 24512 as an adjective).

24

It was the duty of the prefect to convey to the Emperor accounts of the deliberations of the senate and of the proceedings of the assembly of the people, including their *acclamationes* (cf. **9.** 4, **10.** 2): these accounts were sent periodically as a matter of routine. The Emperor has now asked that special excerpts from these accounts should be made in order to gather together the utterances of Praetextatus before the two bodies, and Symmachus sends them with a covering letter.

Per vices mensium singulorum ad perennitatis vestrae scrinia senatus et populi acta mittuntur, quae poterunt indicare, quid vir praecelsae et inlustris memoriae Praetextatus vel ad amplissimum ordinem vel ad devotum vobis populum pro saeculi vestri commendatione pertulerit, ddd. imppp. Valentiniane Theodosi et Arcadi inclyti victores ac triumphatores semper Augusti, (2) sed quia speciatim sacris litteris imperastis, ut, si qua ab eo Romae in his coetibus gesta sunt, agenti in rebus excerpta tradantur, misi omnia iussis caelestibus obsecutus, quae ipso praesente*a* venerabilium orationum vestrarum sanctio definivit et patrum probavit auctoritas; praeterea quae apud plebem locutus est, ut cunctos in amorem bonorum temporum provocaret, adiunxi. 3. iudicium vero civium, quod supremo die de virtute atque innocentia eius habuerunt, speciatim v. c. et inlustri officiorum magistro subditis exemplaribus gestorum intimavi, licet vehiculo publico cum ceteris, quae ex more mittuntur, omnia necesse sit rursus ad serenitatis vestrae notitiam pervenire.

a praesidente *Meyer*: praefante *Mommsen*

Every month, as the months come and go, the proceedings of the senate and people are sent to your Perennities' record-office; they will indicate to you the contribution which, to the greater glory of your age, Praetextatus,[1] of pre-eminent and illustrious memory, made to the most noble order and to a people devoted to you, my Lords Emperors Valentinian, Theodosius, and Arcadius, renowned winners of victories and triumphs, for ever Augusti. 2. But in an imperial dispatch you particularly ordered that whatever he did at Rome in these assemblies should be extracted from the rest and handed to your *agens in rebus*. Obeying your divine commands I sent accounts of the occasions at which he had been present when your authoritative and much-respected dispatches declared your rulings and a responsible senate expressed its approbation. In addition I have attached what he said in addressing the popular assembly with a view to stimulating all to an affection for these blessed times. 3. But I made a special point of acquainting the *magister officiorum* with the strong feelings which on the day he died the citizens expressed about his high qualities and his innocence,[2] and I submitted copies of the proceedings. I know, of course, that all this will travel by imperial post together with the rest of the routine communications and so will come twice to the notice of your Serenities.

[1] See above, 10 n. 1.   [2] An example of an *acclamatio*.

25

25 and **26** should be read together. The affair is spoken of by Symmachus as 'the basilica and the bridge' (§ 2); the two are coupled together, presumably because they were entrusted to the same architect-engineer, but the dispute concerned only the bridge.

Some time before 382 Gratian decided to build a new bridge over the Tiber, north of the Aventine: it was later known as *pons Theodosii*; Cyriades was put in charge, and later Auxentius. The bridge was nearly completed, with a longer span and a shorter span in position. In 382 (winter) part of it collapsed (**26.** 4, 5). The work was then stopped, for the available money or credit was exhausted. (Projects of this kind were financed by the Emperor who made money available in a designated city-fund from which the engineer could draw for materials and labour.) By this time Cyriades and Auxentius were on bad terms, accusing each other of negligence. Probably at the beginning of 383, the Emperor ordered Auchenius Bassus, then prefect of the city, to hold an inquiry (§ 2).

In 383 Valentinian II instructed Sallustius Aventius, now prefect, to set on foot the reconstruction of the basilica of St. Paul-without-the-Walls: of this too Auxentius was in charge.

Bassus held the inquiry and seems to have favoured Auxentius. But about the same time, Cyriades was required by the Emperor to clear himself of the accusations made against him, and to indict those whom he thought responsible for the mismanagement (§ 1). He named Auxentius. Thereupon further inquiry was made by Sallustius Aventius, which passed to Symmachus when he succeeded as prefect (§ 2). He called in *magistri fabrilis artis* to help him to review the reports already made, the estimates, money expended, and the damage (§ 2). After a few days, members of his department reported that Auxentius had disappeared. Thereupon Cyriades asked Symmachus to report to the Emperor (§ 3). Symmachus then sent **25**, to which the Emperor replied at once (**26.** 3) that he was to continue the inquiry with the Vicar to aid him; Aphrodisius was now appointed to succeed Auxentius. At this point **26** was sent.

Iam pridem rescriptum numinis vestri Cyriades v. c. comes et mechanicae professor exhibuit, ddd. imppp., quo statuerat aeternitas vestra, ut se ipse a quorundam criminatione purgaret ac rursus urgueret obiectis, si quos fraudis incesseret. 2. qui cum Auxentium v. c. sub examine decessoris mei coepisset arguere, postquam ad cognitionem meam ventum est, super basilicae atque pontis inmodico sumptu Auxentii v. c. voce perstrictus est, quem Cyriades vir parilis dignitatis mutua accusatione credidit remordendum. visum est igitur adcommodum, ut utriusque aedificationem fida aestimaret inspectio. dedi negotium sollicitis,[a] quantum arbitror, viris et Cyriade paene recusante decrevi fabrilis artis magistros, quos adversario aequiores putabat, aestimationi operis admovendos, manente nihilominus penes Auxentium cura atque administratione coeptorum, quod necdum aeternitas vestra officium eius successore mutasset. 3. itaque exactis aliquot diebus et adhuc pendente operis examine apparitio, quae Auxentio fuerat deputata, per no*t*oriam[b] mihi fecit indicium, deseruisse clarissimum virum susceptorum curam locorum et sub ipso aestatis exordio, quo poss*et* provectus aedificationis adsurgere, nihilum promoveri; sed quia senatoris fuga non videbatur temere credenda, ut inpensius requireretur, admonui. diu nusquam gentium deprehensus, ubi comitatum sacrum numinis vestri adire iussus est, evolavit. interea Cyriades v. c. comes et mechanicus, cum

[a] *Seeck suggests* sollertibus   [b] *Juretus*: notarium *MSS.*

Cyriades, of the distinguished order of senators, *comes* and consultant engineer, long ago displayed, my Lords Emperors, a rescript of your Divinities, in which your Eternities had given a ruling that he himself should clear himself of the charges brought by certain people, and that in turn he should press on with the charges against anyone he was accusing of fraud. 2. In the inquiry held by my immediate predecessor[1] he had begun his arraignment of Auxentius, of the distinguished order of senators; the case came to me to be heard. Cyriades was attacked by Auxentius, of the distinguished order of senators, in person on the matter of the excessive cost of the basilica and the bridge; Cyriades, who held the same rank, then thought that Auxentius ought to receive a bite in return, in the form of a counter-charge. It seemed fitting, then, that a trustworthy inspection should appraise the building work for which each of the two was responsible. I handed the task to some men who, as far as I judged, were conscientious.[2] Cyriades practically refused to accept them, and so I decreed that certain experts in construction, whom Cyriades regarded as fairer to his opponent, should be brought in to appraise the work; all the same the oversight and the administration of the works already started remained with Auxentius since your Eternities had not yet appointed a successor to relieve him of his duties. 3. A few days passed; the examination was not yet concluded when the staff assigned to Auxentius disclosed to me by formal notice that the distinguished senator (*Auxentius*) had abandoned the supervision of the sites he had taken over and that, with the summer about to begin when progress in building could be speeded up, there was no advance whatever. Now, since I thought I could not believe off-hand that a senator had taken to flight, I directed that he should be looked for more carefully. After a long search he could not be apprehended anywhere; when he was ordered to present himself to your Divinities' *comitatus*[3] he fled. Meantime Cyriades, of the distinguished order of senators, *comes* and engineer, saw that my decree had been evaded, and became very anxious lest his

[1] Sallustius Aventius. See above, 23 n. 8.
[2] See Seeck's emendation: perhaps these are the same men as the *magistri* of the next sentence.   [3] A collective term for the imperial court.

SYMMACHI RELATIONES

statutum meum discessu eius videret elusum, multum anxius, ne quid in absentem adversarius moliatur, ut aeternitati vestrae et relationem v. c. prodecessoris mei et nunc acta suggererem, depoposcit. 4. cui audientiam negare non potui, eadem via praecepto numinis vestri cupiens edoceri, quid facto usus sit de aestimatione sumptuum, quos utriusque insumpsit expensio; siquidem meum spectat officium lacunam pecuniae publicae non tacere. fidem litteris sociata gesta praestabunt. quae ubi ad sacras aures perennitatis vestrae recitata pervenerint, oro atque obsecro, ut incertum animi mei responsis imperialibus instruatur.

26

This dispatch follows up 25, which §§ 1 and 2 summarize. §§ 3 to the end carry events a stage further. But the matter dragged on till after Symmachus had retired; a new inquiry was undertaken by Bonosus, of whom Symmachus had a high opinion.

Certum est quidem, clementiam vestram fidei amore et studio veritatis in examen adsiduum saepe explorata revocare, ddd. imppp., sed cum Auxentius v. c. et Cyriades comes ac mechanicus parilis dignitatis quadam inter se concertatione dissentiunt, nonnihil superioribus iudicibus

opponent should intrigue behind his back and asked that I should furnish your Eternities with the report of my predecessor but one, of the distinguished order of senators, and an account of the present proceedings. 4. I could not refuse him a hearing: I hoped in the same way to be instructed by your Divinities' ruling what was the practice in building operations with regard to the assessment of the costs which the outlay made by each of the two had incurred; for it concerns my office closely not to keep silent about a deficiency in the public funds. The proceedings in association with the documents will give you a faithful version. When these are read to you and reach the sacred ears of your Perennities I beg and beseech that my uncertainty of mind may be instructed by an imperial reply.

[*Introduction to* 26 *continued*]

He enlisted the aid of Cyriades, in whom Symmachus had now lost confidence; indeed he urged Eusignius, the praetorian prefect, not to let Cyriades be judge and on trial at the same time (*Ep.* 4. 70, 5. 76). When the bridge was finished is not known.

It is certain that your Clemencies keep under constant review matters often investigated; such is your love of good faith and your eagerness for truth, my Lords Emperors. When Auxentius, of the distinguished order of senators, and Cyriades, *comes* and civil engineer, of the same rank, disagree and quarrel, it is a reflection on those who heard them in the courts earlier. 2. A little

derogatur. 2. iam dudum enim v. c. et inlustris Auchenius Bassus novi pontis opere perspecto sub actorum confectione signavit culpam vel diligentiam singulorum; denuo successor eius eadem loca rimatus adseritur; dehinc cum apud me ex rescripto, quod Cyriades v. c. impetravit, recidiva cognitione confligerent atque ipsis *i*nsistentibus*ᵃ* censuissem, ut utriusque tam sumptus quam aedificationem investigatio discussionis inquireret, v. c. Auxentius repente deseruit iudicatum.

3. de cuius facto missurus relationem, quam sollicitudo intermissi operis exigebat, alia numinis vestri decreta rursus accepi, quibus examini meo v. c. et laudabilem vicarium copulastis, ut utroque residente accusata pontis vitia quaererentur. nec obsequium defuit imperatis. itaque adhibito v. c. tribuno et notario Aphrodisio, cui post Auxentium v. c. novarum molitionum cura legata est, habita est de *i*is quaestio, qui pontis eiusdem fundamenta posuerunt,

4. atque ita constitit, partem brevem atque discretam sub exordio hiemis inchoatam vi fluminis corruisse, cuius inpendium viginti solidorum definitione artifices aestimarunt. sed casus partis istius utpote adhuc a cetero corpore segregatae nihil videtur iniuriae locis distantibus adtulisse; *ip*sam*ᵇ* facili aedificatione reparandam Cyriades v. c. pollicetur. 5. post haec alterius loci exploratio hiulcam conpagem lapidum deprehendit, quam Cyriades comes et mechanicus consilio suo et ratione artis ita positam suggerebat, ut infuso postea inpensarum liquore hiantia stringerentur. quod cum facere debuisset succedentis in-

---

ᵃ Seeck: consistentibus *MSS.*   *ᵇ Mommsen*: quam *MSS.*

while ago Auchenius Bassus, of the distinguished order of senators and an *illustris*, kept under watch the building of the new bridge and, as the contractors finished their work, he made a record of items of faulty or careful execution; his successor is said to have examined most searchingly the same sites over again. In accordance with the imperial rescript which Cyriades, of the distinguished order of senators, asked for and obtained, I reopened the inquiry; they were still in conflict, and when at their insistence I had decided that an investigation involving an audit should inquire into the expenditure and the building-construction of both of them, Auxentius, of the distinguished order of senators, failed to turn up at the court.

3. I was about to send you the report of his behaviour which anxiety about the interruption of the work demanded, when I received new decrees from your Divinities. In them you attached the Vicar, of the distinguished order of senators and highly to be commended, to the examination I was holding so that we should both sit in court[1] and hear the inquiry into the alleged faults in the bridge. Your commands were obeyed. So we called in Aphrodisius, of the distinguished order of senators and *tribunus et notarius*, for, in succession to Auxentius, of the distinguished order of senators, he had been given the responsibility of new building-works. Questions were then put to the men who had laid the foundations of this same bridge.

4. It was established that a length of the bridge, short and standing by itself, had been begun at the beginning of the winter and had collapsed under the impact of the river. Craftsmen estimated the cost of repair at twenty gold coins, at the outside. But the collapse of this part, which was as yet separated from the rest of the structure, did not seem to have damaged in any way the more distant sites. Cyriades, of the distinguished order of senators, assured us that it would not be a difficult building operation to repair it. 5. A second site was examined, and a block of stonework was discovered with gaps in it. Cyriades, *comes* and civil engineer, giving us the advice of his specialist knowledge, told us that the stones had been set in this way so that material could be run in later and the parts separated by gaps would thus be bound together. His successor in the work ought to have taken great care to do this, but he was said, instead of doing it, to have

[1] Cf. **23.** 5, 13.

dustria, adfectasse potius dicitur, ut in auctoris invidiam patula quaeque faeni et sparti manipulis clauderentur. quod cum adstrueret recitatione gestorum, factum quidem urinandi artifex non negavit, sed ex usu operis, non in dehonestamentum Cyriadis c. v. adserebat remedium huiusmodi esse provisum.

6. tunc responsionum varietate conmoti coercuimus a praeteritis discrepantem; at ille Cyriadem sibi ait dudum fuisse terrori. quod credibile non videtur, cum illius temporis cognitor ad fidem veri districta quaestione pervenerit. interea Cyriades v. c. facilem profectum esse suggessit operis sarciendi, cuius stabilitatem, sicuti adsertum est, hiems tertia non resolvit. 7. ipse autem de aedificationibus Auxentii v. c. et de usurpatione inmodici auri nonnulla iudiciis intimavit, quae ideo gestorum paginis placuit adplicari, ut aeternitas vestra cunctis per ordinem patienter auditis providere dignetur, quem ad modum concertantium aemulatione conpressa et integritati sumptuum et firmitati operis consulatur.

contrived that the open places should be filled with bales of hay and esparto so as to bring the originator of the work into discredit. He supported this by quoting from the record of work done and a skilled diver did not deny that that was what had been done, but he said that it was in accordance with normal building practice, and not with a view to dishonouring Cyriades, of the distinguished order of senators, that this kind of measure had been adopted.

6. Disturbed by the varied nature of these answers we 'coerced'[2] this man who took a view different from what had been said in the past; but he said that he had long been in terror of Cyriades. All this seems incredible, for the examiner of that earlier time after a very severe inquiry arrived at a trustworthy account of the truth. Meantime Cyriades, of the distinguished order of senators, gave it as his opinion that progress could easily be made in repairing the work; its stability, as indeed was stated, had not been damaged by the third winter. 7. Of his own accord he furnished some information to the courts about the works carried out by Auxentius, of the distinguished order of senators, and about the appropriation of an excessive amount of gold; this information we decided to attach to the papers of the proceedings so that your Eternities, when you have read them through in order, may think it necessary to consider how the rivalry of these quarrelling men may be stopped and how the expenditure may best be made good and the bridge be firmly built.

[2] That is, exercised the magistrates' powers of *coercitio*.

27

As in **22** Symmachus asks how inconsistent imperial pronouncements are to be reconciled.

Valentinian I ordered in 368 that an *archiatrus* should be appointed for each of twelve out of the fourteen districts of Rome. A vacancy was to be filled not by influence or the word of a magistrate but by election of the doctors; the name of the person recommended was to be referred to the Emperor (*CTh*. 13. 3. 8).

Vt vestri numinis veneror sanctiones, ita observantiam iugem saluberrimis divi genitoris vestri inpendo decretis. quid enim ille constituit, quod possit publica cura deserere? is inter alia, quae in bonum publicum contulit, etiam medendi professoribus dedit ordinem successionis, si locum quempiam decedentis fortuna nudasset. qua lege cautum est, ut primi artis eiusdem de novorum scientia iudicarent. hanc formam, quantum adserunt, aetas secuta servavit, ddd. imppp.

2. nunc Iohannes v. p. non eum gradum, quem subrogandis dederunt scita divalia, sed summo proximum conatur adipisci fultus palatinae militiae privilegio et impetratione specialis oraculi, quo Epicteti archiatri locum tunc adhuc superstitis inpetravit. sed quia lege et more cogentibus summates eiusdem professionis par fuit in examen acciri, adhibitum est iudicio collegium omne medicorum. 3. quorum potissimi inter venerationem legis et novi beneficii reverentiam iudicare non ausi eum locum Iohanni v. p. statuerunt deferendum, quem tenere potuisset, si eo tempore, quo aulae obsequiis deputatus est, archiatrorum numero fuisset

Two years later it was added that not less than seven doctors should make the necessary promotions and then the new appointment should be placed last (13. 3. 9).

John, a *perfectissimus*, presented himself in Rome alleging he had an imperial appointment to the second highest post in the medical service at Rome. Consulted by Symmachus, the doctors put forward alternative views as to what should be done.

I have the utmost respect for the directives of your Divinities; no less do I accord never-failing regard to the most wholesome decrees of a former Emperor, your father. For he never made any decision which anyone caring for the state could neglect. Among his other contributions to the public good he prescribed the order of succession for the profession of medicine, if the chances which cause a man to vacate a post had left a place open.[1] By this law it was provided that the leaders in this same profession should express their own judgement about the skill of new applicants. This procedure, so it is said, was observed in the era that followed, my Lords Emperors.

2. But now John, a *perfectissimus*, is attempting to obtain not the grade which the divine decrees assigned to new appointments, but the grade next to the top. He is relying on special consideration as a member of the court civil service, and on the possession of an individual pronouncement which granted him the position of Epictetus, a state doctor, while he was still alive. Now, since law and custom compelled, it was right that the leaders of the profession should be summoned to an inquiry, and I had the whole college of doctors up to my court. 3. The most influential of them, torn between respect for the law and regard for this new grant, did not venture to pass any judgement, but decided that the post should be given to John, a *perfectissimus*, which he would have been able to hold if he had been attached to the panel of state doctors at the time when he was in fact

---

[1] See introductory note.

adiunctus. *s*ed cum ab eo palatini honoris indicia poscerentur, ut codicillorum praerogativa monstraret, quis illi inter archiatros ordo conpeteret, adseruit domestica expilatione etiam documenta dignitatis ablata. 4. at vero pars magna medicorum munita lege divali eorum exempla deprompsit, qui e palatio in hunc gradum[a] servato ordine transierunt. quare motus ambiguis et neque divi genitoris vestri ausus rumpere sanctionem neque obviam specialibus venire praeceptis, divino arbitrio numinis vestri subditis allegationibus partium summam negotii reservavi, opperiens, quid deliberatio augusta constituat, cui soli fas est de scitis divalibus iudicare.

[a] *Seeck suggests* in hunc locum graduum

appointed to the service of the court.[2] But, when he was asked for proof of his office at court, so that his title of appointment might show what rank among the state doctors was to be regarded as due to him, he alleged that his house had been burgled and the papers proving his office had been taken away. 4. But a large number of the doctors, relying on the law of a former Emperor, cited as precedents men who had passed from the court into this place (*Rome*), without upsetting the order of promotion. And so, disturbed by these conflicting views and not venturing to contravene the decree of your father nor to counter a special directive, I have left the last word in this matter to the divine judgement of your Divinities; I have attached the statements of the parties and I await what your august counsels may decide, for only they have the right to pass judgement when the decrees of a former Emperor are concerned.

[2] He should receive such seniority at Rome as the original date of his appointment to the civil service warranted.

28

Scirtius had been ejected from land of which he had possession; he said he had been wrongfully ejected and claimed reinstatement. ['Possession' means occupancy, and Roman law insisted that everything should be put back into the state existing before the *invasio*, and then the rights of the possession would be determined.] Symmachus recognized that an appeal from a *praeiudicium* was not allowed (for reinstatement was not a judicial case, but an interdict by a magistrate). But he does send on the appeal and gives his reasons (§ 1); perhaps the identity of the prime mover in the case was another reason. This person was Olybrius, who remains in the background and uses others as his tools. Through his agent he resisted the reinstatement of Scirtius and carried off local inhabitants who on Symmachus' orders were being escorted to Rome. Symmachus concentrated on obtaining witnesses of 'possession'. Olybrius pushed in the heirs of Theseus to oppose Scirtius: only one witness appeared, a freedman said to have been freed by Theseus. He said some residents on the estate hid, others were carried off to Olybrius' villa. The councillors of Praeneste were summoned: at last the *procurator* of Olybrius had to appear, for the evidence compelled it.

Scirtius now had to contend against him and the heirs of Theseus (§ 5). Examination of the councillors established that Scirtius paid the land-tax and was therefore *possessor*: thus Symmachus pronounced. The *procurator* now claimed that Olybrius had acquired half the land as a result of the death of Theseus. The question then arose whether Scirtius had given half to Theseus and half to Theseus' heirs, or half to Theseus and his heirs. Symmachus thought Scirtius meant to retain half for himself, and he went on to consider the matter as one of ownership. Appeal was made, which Symmachus now sent on.

On 29 November 384 a constitution was made allowing appeals from a *praeiudicium*. This dispatch must therefore be dated before them (so also **16**), while **33** was written after that date. The constitution, which is in general terms, was addressed to Symmachus (*CTh.* 11. 30. 44).

Quid possint iusti principes culpare, praesentio: in causis etenim, quibus momenti reformatio postulatur, appellationes recipi non oportet.

sed consulto nunc obiectum provocationis admisi, ut in examen clementiae vestrae et invasionis indignitas et modus iudicii perveniret, ddd. imppp.

2. nam Scirtius v. p. ereptam sibi partem Caesarianae massae crebra aditione conquestus, cum integrationem status, quem amiserat, inpetrasset, heredes Thesei, qui reluctarentur, obiecti sunt, du*m* rever*a* Artemisius Olybri clarissimi atque inlustris viri actor executur*o*, ut ipse professus est, obviavit, et cum ad pernoscendum possessionis statum loci habitatores adesse iussissem, in iniuriam legum Rufino officiali iussa curanti, qui deducebantur, abrepti sunt. gesta indicabunt facti incivilis auctores. interea distuli vindictam iudiciorum et rursus officio negotium dedi, ut necessarios evocaret.

3. tunc cessantibus actoribus clarissimae domus ceterisque subtractis ad contradicendum Thesei subrogantur heredes, uno tantum exhibiti,[a] qui se adsereret libertum esse defuncti. is interrogatus, quo abissent incolae praediorum, delituisse nonnullos, Scirti vero mancipia ad *su*b*u*rbanam villam, quae est clarissimi et inlustris viri Olybrii, translata respondit.

---

[a] *Seeck suggests that* ceterisque (*sc.* testibus) subtractis *should be placed after* heredes *and proposes* unus tantum exhibitus

I know in advance the criticism just Emperors can make of me; in suits in which reinstatement in possession is demanded, appeals ought not to be allowed.

But I have deliberately admitted an appeal, which, of course, stays proceedings, so that a disgraceful case of trespass, together with my method of adjudicating, may be brought to you for your examination, my Lords Emperors.

2. Scirtius, a man of *perfectissimus* rank, frequently attended my court to complain that he had been robbed of a portion of the 'Caesarian' estates; at his request I restored the possession to him which he had lost. Thereupon the heirs of Theseus were put forward as objectors to fight the award of reinstatement; but in actual fact Artemisius, who was employed as agent by Olybrius[1] of the distinguished order of senators and an *illustris*, refused entry, as he himself admitted, to the official who was going to effect the reinstatement. With a view to establishing the exact situation with regard to possession, I ordered the people who lived at the place to appear before me. My official Rufinus was carrying out my commands when, in defiance of the law, the people who were being brought to the court were seized from his custody. The proceedings of the case will show who was responsible for this barbaric act. Meantime I put off sentence of punishment by the courts for this, and again I gave my department the task of summoning the necessary witnesses.

3. The agents of the distinguished house still hung back, and the heirs of Theseus were put forward in their place to make a counterplea; and, since the other witnesses had been removed, only one was produced in court, whose purpose was to state that he was the freedman of the deceased (*Theseus*). On being asked where the inhabitants of the estates had gone, he replied that some had hidden but that Scirtius' slaves had been carried off to the suburban villa belonging to Olybrius, of the distinguished order

[1] Quintus Clodius Hermogenianus Olybrius, a Christian and of Christian family; shared the anti-senatorial policy of Valentinian I; married daughter of Auchenius Bassus. Career in Dess. 1271; consular of Campania (before 361), proconsul of Africa 361-2, *praefectus urbi* 368-70, *praefectus praetorio* of Illyricum and later of the Oriens 379-80; character, Amm. 28. 4. 1. By his marriage he became related to Petronius Probus, for whom see Amm. 27. 11. 1 f.

cetera ut a liberto Thesei dicta praetereo, licet in eum praescriptio ista non conpetat, cum a patre minorum beneficium libertatis acceperit.

4. his ita positis Praenestini curiales, quorum in regione Caesariana possessio iacet, missis apparitoribus exhibentur. tunc demum v. c. et spectabilis Olybrii procurator emergit *tandem cogentibus indiciis postulatus*;[b] adest etiam defensor minorum. Scirtio adversum duos pugna proponitur, quamvis patrocinia clarissimae domus et successorum Thesei quadam specie dissiderent.

5. itur in quaestionem possessionis; quae partium variis agitata conflictibus ad interrogationem testium iure transivit. admoveri singillatim, ut mos est, iubeo curiales; nominum et dignitatis ab uno quoque posco responsa; tunc locorum iustos possessores require; dehinc percontor, quis annuas functiones aut indicta persolverit. cum secundum Scirtium testimonia cuncta procederent atque eam possessionem cum Theseo tenuisse constaret, quando et per quos deiectus esset examino. secundum fere vel tertium mensem manere consentiunt, ut eum clarissimae atque inlustris domus homines expulerunt. 6. auditis optimatum testimoniis denuo cum defensoribus admitto iurgantes; quaesita et responsa partibus intimantur. ibi Tarpeius v. c. procurator inlustris viri Olybrii adseruit, ei sex uncias praediorum Thesei morte quaesitas. contra Scirtius de sex unciis, quas minores etiam se consentiente retinebant, non ibat infitias nec sua interesse dicebat, actores clarissimae domus an heredes Thesei eadem parte fruerentur.

[b] *transposed by Seeck*: *after* minorum *MSS.*

of senators and an *illustris*. I refrain from quoting the rest of what he said because he was a freedman,[2] though the ban on his evidence which is familiar to you does not apply, since he received the gift of freedom from the father of the minors.

4. With these points established, servants of the court were dispatched and members of the town council of Praeneste were produced in court; the Caesarian estate lies in their district. Then at last the *procurator* of Olybrius, of the distinguished order of senators and a *spectabilis*, came out into the open; his presence had at last been demanded by the compelling nature of the evidence; also counsel for the minors was present. Scirtius therefore had to fight on two fronts, though, in fact, the barristers for the distinguished house and those appearing for Theseus' successors were in some respects at variance.

5. We passed then to an examination of the actual possession; it was conducted amid much conflict of different kinds waged by the parties and it then rightly passed on to the questioning of witnesses. I ordered that the councillors should be brought before me one by one, as is usual. I asked each one to tell me in reply what was his name and rank. I asked who were the rightful possessors, and after that I inquired who paid the annual taxes and the levy.[3] All the evidence went in favour of Scirtius: it was clear that he had held possession jointly with Theseus. So I investigated to find out when and by whom he had been ejected. They agreed that two or three months ago, men from the distinguished and illustrious house had expelled him from the property. 6. After hearing the testimony of the leading men I again admitted the litigants with their barristers; the questions and answers were made known to them. At this point Tarpeius, of the distinguished order of senators, *procurator* of Olybrius, of illustrious rank, affirmed that Olybrius had obtained half of the estates on the death of Theseus. Then Scirtius, in reply, said that he made no denial in the matter of the half which the minors, with his agreement, retained in their possession and that it did not matter to him whether the agents of the distinguished house or the heirs of Theseus enjoyed possession of that part.

---

[2] He could not be examined to the disadvantage of his patron.

[3] The chief *functio* was probably the *capitatio*, a tax on every 'head', owner, family, workers, animals. If in a province it was found that the annual budget was insufficient, the Emperor ordered an *indictio* of whatever goods were necessary to the government, as e.g. grain, clothing, meat.

7. tunc actionibus copulatis Scirtium urguere coeperunt, quod secundum mandatum c. m. feminae Farianae sex uncias Theseo per epistulam reddidisset,[c] sex vero alias in eius liberos contulisset spontanea largitate. ad haec Scirtius idem litteris familiaribus quod donationibus in Theseum vel parvulos transfusum esse dicebat ipsius petitu, ut actorum fides beneficium roboraret. et re vera cum posteriora gesta pro indiviso sex uncias massae in eos conlatas esse testentur, intelleximus partem donatoris exceptam. cur enim pro indiviso daret, si nihil resederat, quod ipse retineret?

8. sed haec cum ad proprietatis causam dicerem pertinere, recitata est a defensoribus constitutio, quae iudicibus tribuit copiam, non inponit necessitatem, ut quotiens de possessione successionis iudicant, continuo, si casus tulerit, etiam de iure cognoscant. qua actione confessi sunt ad aliam causam se malle transire. praeterea non solus Scirtius proprietatis quaestione videbatur urguendus, cum ipsi quoque inter se super hac parte quodammodo dissiderent.

9. quare de possessione secundum documenta Scirtii et principalium testimonia iudicavi, adversariis eius sex unciarum retentione et iure firmatis; principalem vero causam salvis allegationibus partium futuro examini reservavi, et mox sententiae exemplar emisi, cum eius editionem procurator spectabilis viri continuo postulasset.

10. tunc Scirtius optulit sanctiones, quibus doceret in reformatione momenti nullum esse appellationibus locum. postridie procurator clarissim*i* et inlustris *viri*[d] ac defensor minorum, qui putaba*n*tur[d] in iudicio discrepare, concordiam

[c] tradidisset Mommsen, *which has been translated.*   [d] *Bethmann-Hollweg*

7. Then the two parties, combining their cases, began to press Scirtius, saying that according to a mandate of Fariana, of the distinguished order of senators, now deceased, Scirtius had handed over half to Theseus by letter; the other half he had conferred on Theseus' children as a voluntary act of generosity. In reply Scirtius said that the land transferred by letter was the same as the land transferred by deed of gift to Theseus or the young children; (he had written the letter) at Theseus' request so that his act of kindness might be attested by the trustworthiness of documents. Now, when as a matter of fact later proceedings show that half of the property had been conferred on Theseus or the young children as an indivisible whole, I realized that the part belonging to the donor was outside these transactions. For why would he give away property as an indivisible whole, if nothing remained over for him to keep for himself?

8. I then said that the case now raised the question of ownership; the barristers for the defence read out a constitution which gave judges the power, but imposed no obligation, to go on to examine right of ownership, if necessity arose, in trials concerned with possession of inheritance. By this action they admitted that they preferred to change their ground and take up another issue. Besides it was not only Scirtius who was likely to be embarrassed by an inquiry into ownership; for on this matter they themselves were to some extent at variance.

9. And so I gave judgement along the lines of Scirtius' statements and the evidence of the leading men of Praeneste, with his opponents confirmed in legal retention of one half. I kept the allegations made by both parties and reserved for future examination the main issue of the case, and presently I sent out a copy of my judgement, since the *procurator* of the man of *spectabilis* rank had immediately demanded its publication.

10. Then Scirtius cited in objection certain enactments by means of which he urged that in a case of reinstatement of possession no room was given for appeal. On the next day the *procurator* of the man who was of the distinguished order of senators and an *illustris*, and the barrister appearing for the minors, who seemed in court to be on different sides, revealed

suam iunctis provocationibus indicarunt. 11. haec est omnis summa luctaminis; nunc oraculum numinis vestri fortuna litis expectat. gesta et supplementa partis utriusque subieci; quibus instructa perennitas vestra exemplo unius causae securitati omnium dignabitur commodare.

28 SYMMACHI RELATIONES

that they really had been acting in association by making joint appeal. This is a résumé of the whole struggle: now the issue of the case awaits a pronouncement by your Divinities. I attach the proceedings and the supplementary statements of both parties. Equipped with these your Perennities will think fit, by setting a precedent in one case, to serve the cause of everybody's peace of mind.

29

The *arca vinaria*, which sold wine at a reduced rate to the people, accumulated quantities of small coins: these it exchanged for gold *solidi* presented by the money-changers. The exchange-rate no longer took into account the rise in the value of gold. Symmachus asks for it to be revised. For his care for the interests of the guilds cf. **14, 20**.

Vendendis solidis, quos plerumque publicus usus exposcit, collectariorum corpus obnoxium est, quibus arca vinaria statutum pretium subministrat. huic hominum generi taxationis exiguae vilitate nutanti divus frater numinis vestri tantum pro singulis solidis statuit conferendum, quantum aequitas illius temporis postulabat, ddd. imppp. sed paulatim auri enormitate crescente vis remedii divalis infracta est, et cum in foro venalium rerum maiore summa solidus censeatur, nummulariis pretia minora penduntur.

2. petunt igitur de aeternitate vestra pro ratione praesenti ius*t*a definitionis augmenta, qui iam tanto oneri sustinendo pares esse non possunt. haec est causa querimoniae, quam divinis sensibus vestris fides gestorum plenius intimabit; si petitionis genus probabile iudicatis, quaeso ut huic quoque parti praecepto mansuetudinis vestrae salubre remedium deferatur.

The guild of money-changers is responsible for selling gold *solidi* (*to the government*), for the public need for the most part demands them. The treasury of the *arca vinaria* pays the money-changers a fixed price. When this class of people was about to collapse because the miserable rate of exchange brought them a low return, the late brother[1] of your Divinities decided that as much was to be given to them for each *solidus* as a fair deal at that time demanded, my Lords Emperors. But, as the value of gold, already high, gradually increased, the effect of the late Emperor's remedy was impaired and, as in the commodity market the *solidus* is valued at a higher sum, relatively smaller prices are paid to the changers.

2. They petition your Eternities that, to take the place of the present formula, there should be a fair increase in the rates prescribed; and indeed already they cannot shoulder the great burden they have to bear. This is the reason for their complaint, which will be amplified for your divine sensibilities in the faithful account of the proceedings. If you judge that this kind of complaint may be approved, I ask that by a decree of your Graces this party too may be granted a remedy which will save them from their plight.

[1] Gratian.

30

This dispatch asks for guidance in a case in which a special pronouncement by the Emperor and the normal legal processes of administration are in conflict. Fiscal cases concerning *clarissimi* went direct to the *praefectus urbi*.

Palatini munerationum sacrarum Avitus et Castor quaestus publicos eruentes inter cetera nomina, quae iudicio persequuntur, heredes Postumiani c. m. v. in examen meum conventionibus evocarunt, ddd. imppp., Luciano monente, qui census senatorios ante tractavit, quod oblativis functionibus eadem domus esset obnoxia. pars debiti Lollianam, pars Cattianillam pariter ac Severillam suggerebatur urgere. 2. interea sequestrato Lollianae c. f. nomine, quam pro sex unciis stringit exactio, harum orta refragatio est, quas pro singulis bonorum quadrantibus solutionis cura mordebat. conperendinato plerumque iudicio res eo deducta est, ut fisci patrocinium securitates a clarissimis personis inpleti per vices muneris flagitaret, Cattianillae vero ac Severillae defensio rescripto ad relationem divi principis niteretur.
3. vetus enim quaestio et cognitionibus praefecturae frequenter agitata usque ad inclyti semperque verendi genitoris vestri cucurrit arbitrium, qui Viventii clarissimae et inlustris memoriae viri tunc praefecti urbis insinuatione consultus quadam rescripti parte signavit, suis quibusque temporibus a Cattianilla ac Severilla clarissimis feminis oblativa munera soluta constare. 4. hic me *n*odus[a] iam promptum atque declivem ad efflagitanda inlationum documenta defixit, cum videretur omnibus securitatibus esse vehementior imperatoris adsertio. de cuius responsi iugi honore mansuris vestrae

[a] Meyer

Avitus and Castor, secretaries at the imperial office of *munerationes*, in the process of weeding out emoluments enjoyed at public cost, came upon several cases which they are prosecuting in court; among them were the heirs of Postumianus, a member of the distinguished order of senators now dead, whom they have summoned to appear for investigation before me on a series of charges, my Lords Emperors. Lucianus, who formerly handled the census-returns of senators, furnished the information that this family was liable for payment of the *aurum oblaticium*. It was stated that part of the debt was to be borne by Lolliana, and part by Cattianilla and Severilla equally. 2. In the meantime, the case of Lolliana, a woman of the distinguished order of senators, was set aside to be dealt with separately; on her a crushing demand at the rate of half of her property was made. The others put up resistance; they are each experiencing the gnawing anxiety of having to pay at the rate of a quarter of their property. Judgement was frequently delayed, but finally the matter was reduced to this, that the representatives of the fisc demanded receipts to be shown by members of the senatorial order for successive payments of what was due, while the defence for Cattianilla and Severilla placed its reliance on a rescript of the late Emperor in reply to a reference made to him.

3. For this old problem, often argued in judicial inquiries held at this prefecture, ran full course to the final decision of your renowned and always respected father.[1] He it was who, when consulted at the suggestion of the prefect of the city of the time, the late Viventius,[2] of the distinguished order of senators and an *illustris*, signified in a particular passage of a rescript that the payment of the *aurum oblaticium* at the several proper occasions by Cattianilla and Severilla was now established. 4. I am always ready and indeed prone to demand proofs of payment, but this complication made me hold my hand, for I saw that a statement made by an Emperor carried more force than all the receipts in the world. It is right that a final decision about his rescripts, which will remain in never-failing honour, should rest with you; for we have become accustomed to respect rather than to

[1] Valentinian I.
[2] Viventius, a Pannonian and a friend of Valentinian I; *praefectus urbi* October 366 to May 367; *praefectus praetorio Galliarum* 368–71. See Amm. 26. 4. 4, 27. 3. 11 ff. Probably a Christian.

clementiae fas est esse iudicium; nos venerari potius quam interpretari oracula divina consuevimus. praesto sunt monumenta gestorum, partium quoque supplementa non desunt. aequum est, ut maiestatis vestrae informetur arbitrio humana cunctatio.

interpret the pronouncements of Emperors. The record of the proceedings is ready to your hand, and the statements of the parties are also available to fill in the details. It is just that the hesitation to which men are liable should receive directions from the judgement of your Majesties.

31

The normal processes of law have failed to bring Valerianus to judgement; Symmachus asks the Emperor to act.

Moribus scaevis familiare atque cognatum est armare spiritus inpunitatis exemplo, ddd. imppp. cur enim secundum desperet effugium, qui laqueos criminis prioris evasit? praesenti causae congruit praemissa sententia. siquidem Valerianus vir clarissimus, cui lar in Epiro esse suggeritur, neque rescriptorum veneratione neque legum severitate vel pactionum fide aut iudiciorum reverentia permovetur. 2. qui primo in examen praetorianae sedis iussus acciri ad supplicationem v. c. Iunioris vim rescripti, sta*tu*tum praecelsae potestatis elusit; dehinc proconsularibus evocatus edictis leges pari arte frustratus est; nunc cum et actione civili et criminali accusatione premeretur, statutis inciviliter repugnavit, ut apparitores praefecturae urbanae partim notoriis partim suggestione signarunt. quorum unus agente in rebus eo mortuo, ad quem sacri praecepti executio pertinebat, adfectum se a Valeriano gravibus iniuriis indicavit.

3. motus igitur indignitate talium querellarum, cum viderem rursus inludi posse iudiciis, si quid severius censuissem, factu optimum credidi, ut aeternitati vestrae causae istius pontificium reservarem; soli enim iure corrigitis admissa potissimae dignitatis. fides rerum gestis cohaerentibus explicatur; nihilominus adservatu*r* regressus apparitor, qui

To arm arrogance with examples of wrongdoing unpunished is an action which is the family connection, indeed the blood-relation, of clumsy stupidity, my Lords Emperors. If a man has evaded being caught for an earlier crime, why should he abandon hope of a second escape? The foregoing reflection just fits the present case. Valerianus,[1] of the distinguished order of senators, whose home is stated to be in Epirus, is influenced neither by respect for rescripts, nor by the severity of laws, nor by loyalty to agreements, nor by regard for the law courts. 2. To start with, he was ordered to be summoned to the praetorian Bench to attend an inquiry on the petition of Junior, of the distinguished order of senators. He made sport of the compelling power of a rescript and the decree of the supreme magistrate; after that he was summoned to appear by edicts issued by a proconsul; with equal cunning he cheated the law.[2] And now recently, when he was being prosecuted in a civil action and also on a criminal charge, with a discourtesy unbecoming to a citizen he resisted every legal order; to this effect officials of the urban prefecture have made attestations partly by laying information, partly by statement. Indeed one official, after the *agens in rebus* whose duty it was to carry out your sacred directive had died, gave notice that severe injuries had been inflicted on himself by Valerianus.

3. And so I was incensed by the indignity revealed by these complaints; I saw that, if I passed still sterner sentence, a mockery would once again be made of the lawcourts: I therefore thought I should act for the best if I reserved for your Eternities the right of pronouncing in this case.[3] For you alone have the right to punish misdemeanours committed by men of the most powerful rank. The true facts are set out in the proceedings which I attach; all the same, when the official returned who gave news of the senator's arrogant behaviour and the attacks made by his slaves,

---

[1] Valerianus, not to be confused with the *praefectus urbi* of the same name in 383.
[2] Epirus was under a *praeses*: perhaps Valerianus' estates were also in the proconsular province of Achaea.
[3] The law concerning the prefect's role in judging *clarissimi* was repeatedly altered and the exact nature of Symmachus' involvement is disputed. Chastagnol (*Préf.* 126 n. 1) thinks it was because civil charges were also preferred. See 48.

contumaciam senatoris et serviles impetus nuntiavit, suggestionibus suis, cum forte usus tulerit, adfuturus. quaeso aeternam clementiam vestram, ut omnibus solita aequitate perpensis evagari ulterius frustratorem tot iudicum non sinatis.

32

Theodorus prosecuted Flavianus, who resisted by pleading an *exceptio*, that is, that the charge did not apply in the special case; Flavianus and his successor died. Theodorus said a 'renewal of time' should have been granted. The defence replied that only a prosecutor's heir could get a renewal; this plea was denied,

Difficile est, ut bona causa sit, cuius actio in ius alterius desperatione transfertur. id adeo res probavit, ddd. imppp. nam Theodorus, ut adseruit, ex protectoribus ab Anniana quadam in rem suam procurator creatus iam pridem clarissimo atque emendatissimo viro Eupraxio urbanis tribunalibus

I kept him here so that he could support his statements if the need arose. I beg your Eternal Clemencies that, when you have weighed all these matters with your customary fairness, you will not allow a man who has defeated so many magistrates to overstep the mark any longer.

[*Introduction to* 32 *continued*]

a citation being made that either party could get it. Symmachus thinks renewal is irrelevant, for a prosecution against a man cannot be extended so as to lie against another person. He sends on the appeal none the less—perhaps because Flavianus was a *protector*.

It is difficult to see how the cause can be good if in sheer desperation its pleadings are transferred so as to attack the rights of another. This the facts have proved absolutely, my Lords Emperors. Theodorus, of the corps of *protectores*, as he asserts, was appointed by a certain Anniana as agent to look after her property; some time ago he brought a charge against a certain Flavianus in a case summoned for immediate trial; Eupraxius,[1]

---

[1] Flavius Eupraxius, of Mauretania, probably a Christian (Amm. 27. 7. 6). *Magister memoriae* 367; *quaestor sacri palati* (27. 6. 14); *praefectus urbi* 373-4 (28. 1. 25).

praesidente Flavianum quendam denuntiata lite pulsavit, sed diem legitimum causae lapsus excessit. 2. longo intervallo a me petita reparatio cum partes ad necessarium contraxisset examen, post multas allegationes, quas iudicia ut invalidas respuerunt, orta praescriptio est, quae adsereret novari tempora possessore mortuo debuisse; nam constabat non modo Flavianum, qui propositam legibus quaestionem primus exceperat, sed etiam successorem eius finem fecisse vivendi. 3. ad hoc promissa est lectio veluti probatura indiciis, novationem tantum petitoris heredi esse decretam; quod verbo quidem adsertum sed sanctionibus non probatum contrariae legis recitatione conpressum est. secutus igitur scita manifesta et nullis principum vacuata responsis cessare processum negotii iudicavi, cum lis alteri denuntiata aliam personam temporibus novationis etiam exactis tenere non posset. 4. tunc oblatis provocationis libellis suspensa sententia. cuius meritum perennitas vestra lectis gestis ac refutatoriis cohaerentibus aestimabit: ego in referendo prolixus esse non debui, cum paene in ipso actionum vestibulo repulsa legibus causa constiterit.

of the distinguished order of senators and of irreproachable character, was then president of the urban tribunals. There was delay in bringing the case and the day defined by law went past. 2. After a long interval I was petitioned to grant a 'renewal of times', and the parties were brought together for the necessary examination. Many excuses were made which the courts rejected as without substance; then an objection was lodged that a new date ought to have been fixed since the defendant had died. For it was established that not only Flavianus, who in the first instance had objected to the trial proposed by the law on the ground of special circumstances, but also his successor had departed this life. 3. In reply a promise was made that passages of law would be read aloud which would prove, it was alleged, by clear evidence that a renewal of date was allowed by decree only to the heir of a plaintiff.[2] This plea, which was made only on the word of its advocate, and not proved by any legal rulings, was quashed by the citation of a law which ran counter to it.[3] And so I followed decisions which were clear and not made void by 'replies' from emperors, and I gave judgement that the matter should not be taken any further; for a prosecution brought against a party cannot affect a third person especially if dates for renewal have lapsed. 4. At that point a petition of appeal to the Emperor was presented and my judgement was held in abeyance. Its rightness your Perennities will assess when you have read the proceedings and the counter-statements which I attach. In making this reference to you there was no need for me to be diffuse, for almost at the very threshold of the proceedings the case stood defeated at law.

[2] Perhaps *CTh.* 2. 6. 4 (338).
[3] *CTh.* 2. 6. 3 (361) which allows renewal *altero ex litigatoribus in lite defuncto.*

33

This appeal by a *suarius* on a matter of *possessio* would normally have been dealt with by the prefect of the city, but Valentinian II seems for a short time to have taken such cases out of his hands and given them to the *vicarius*. But in this instance the Emperor expressly asked Symmachus to look into it *ex delegatu*, as his representative (cf. 36): the date is after 29 November (see **16, 28**).

In causis appellationum malo ius potestatis infringere quam interpretationum dubia sustinere, praesertim conscius haud iniquae iudicationis, cui nonnihil honoris eveniet, si aeternitatis vestrae oraculo roboretur, ddd. imppp.

2. tuli igitur Constantium suarium temere provocantem, cum ex rescripto numinis vestri statum, quem Theodosio absenti ademerat, reformassem. mota enim vestra clementia supplicationibus quer*u*lis brevi examine iussit inquiri, an Theodosio extra conflictum locato ac deinde, ne rebus excederet, provocante possessionem corporum Constantius esset indeptus. allegata igitur praeceptione divina primo cognitionem totius negotii, quamvis speciatim mihi tranquillitatis vestrae delegatione mandatam, viri clarissimi vicarii praesentiae reservavi. siquidem videbatur haec causa ceteris provocationibus esse coniuncta, quae v. c. prodecesso*ri* meo negabantur admissae et alterum mecum sumpsera*n*t cognitorem.

3. dehinc ubi eam partem, quae ad illius temporis iudicem pertinebat, vestro retinuistis examini, appellationis inquisitione discreta, cum[a] iam participem iudicii non haberem,

---

[a] *Seeck suggests* cum *should be put after* examini

In cases of appeal I prefer to diminish the authority of my office rather than to uphold doubtful attempts at interpretation. Especially I have in mind a not inequitable adjudication which will attract a certain amount of credit, if it is confirmed by a pronouncement of your Eternities, my Lords Emperors.

2. I put up with Constantius, a *suarius*, when he ill-advisedly appealed to the Emperors after I had restored possession of a property which he had taken away from Theodosius while he was away from home; I did this in pursuance of a rescript of your Divinities. For your Clemencies, moved by his plaintive supplications to you, ordered a brief inquiry to be held to discover whether, while Theodosius was situated outside the scene of conflict, and was in process of appealing to the Emperor so that he should not be put out of his property, Constantius had seized possession of his belongings. I therefore declared your divine instructions: at first I reserved the preliminary hearing of the business as a whole till the Vicar, of the distinguished order of senators, could be present, although the hearing had in fact been laid expressly on me by delegation from your Tranquillities. For this case seemed to me to be bound up with all the other appeals which were refused admission to my predecessor but one, of the distinguished order of senators, and had claimed a hearing by a second judge sitting with me.

3. Thereafter, when you retained for your own inquiry that part of the case which belonged to the judge of the earlier occasion, and, since the inquiry about appeal was now separated from the rest of the case, I had not a partner on the bench; and so in

turbatae possessionis querellam rescripto obsecutus audivi; et quia Theodosium iudicio non interfuisse constabat, quo sibi demptas questus est facultates, nec ulla precum mendacia Constantius detegebat, executus sum circa germanum supplicatoris heredem caeleste iudicium reformato statu, quem claruit mox proposita appellatione defensum, licet cultus[b] subditus quaestioni libellos, quos Theodosius publicavit, apud se resedisse memoraverit. nihilominus oboediens imperatis statui, ut fides gestorum superiorum ad augusta scrinia mitteretur. 4. hinc orta est provocatio, cuius vel iustitia vel contumacia sacro expendetur arbitrio. interea constitutionis memor sequestrari mobilia fructusque praecepi, ne medii temporis usurpatio abutatur indebitis. omnium gestorum fida documenta cum supplementis partium relationi ex more sociata sunt, ut diu fluctuanti causae tandem stabilem terminum divino ore ponatis.

[b] cornicularius *or* cognitionalis *Seeck*

obedience to your rescript I heard the complaints about 'interference with possession'. Now, because it was established that Theodosius had not been present in court when he complained that his property was taken away from him, and because Constantius revealed no flaws in his opponent's plea, I carried out your divine judgement in respect of the appellant's brother and heir. I restored possession, which it was clear was resisted since intention to appeal was soon declared. Though the *cornicularius* assigned to the inquiry mentioned that the written indictment which Theodosius made public reposed at his office,[1] none the less, in obedience to your commands, I decided that a true account of the earlier proceedings should be sent to your august record office. 4. This was the origin of the appeal to the Emperor. Your sacred judgement will weigh up its justice or its arrogance. Meanwhile I remembered your imperial constitution, and I gave directions that all the movable goods and the incomings should be sequestrated, so that use of them in the interim should not cause impairment to property not yet awarded to anyone.[2] Faithful minutes of all the proceedings, together with additional statements by the parties, are attached as usual to this dispatch, so that a divine pronouncement by you may at last put a firm end to a case which has been moving this way and that for a long time.

[1] i.e. the *officium urbanum*.   [2] See *Dig.* 49. 1. 21. 3.

34

Apart from 3, this is the most eloquent of the *Relationes*. It was written in the latter part of Symmachus' tenure of office (for it complains bitterly of an attack on his wife and himself), when anti-senatorial feeling had again gathered strength. The story may be briefly reconstructed, with the help of *Ep.* 9. 150 and Amm. 27. 3. 2, 27. 7. 3, as follows; it falls into two parts.

(i) Symmachus married Rusticiana, the daughter of Orfitus, who was twice *praefectus urbi*, in 353–6 and 357–9. He allowed the funds in the *arca vinaria* to become depleted, and defended himself by saying that he had used the money for public buildings. Constantius ordered repayment and added a threat—*comminatio sub condicione*, that is, Orfitus must himself repay or make someone else who was responsible repay—and the *officium urbanum* was included in the threat. It seems that Orfitus and his department did in fact make repayment.

(ii) Again in 360–1, in the prefecture of Tertullus, a shortage in the funds was revealed. But the *comminatio* was held in abeyance till Tertullus could hold an inquiry. The inquiry dragged on for years, and prefect after prefect continued under the threat. At last—apparently on the information of Terentius, a baker[1]—the *comminatio* was made operative against Orfitus in respect of his conduct during his second prefecture. Orfitus no doubt gave the same explanation, but he was condemned to go into exile and his goods were forfeited. He was recalled in 367 and died in 370.

Gratian took up the matter again, 382–3. Auditors working under the direction of the *comes sacrarum largitionum* Basilius were employed, and Auchenius Bassus was responsible for the general inquiry. Gratian insisted that the prefect and his department were to blame. Bassus and his successor as prefect, Sallustius Aventius, discovered—no doubt the auditors discovered this—that 11,446 *solidi* had been paid, but paid to the fisc and not to the *arca vinaria*; the rest, it was held, should be made good by

[1] Terentius governed Thracia Annonaris in 364 (*CTh.* 2. 1. 4). Amm. 27. 3. 1 says he was born at Pistoria in Tuscia, and was rewarded with the governorship for having prosecuted Orfitus for embezzlement.

the prefect and his officials. Documents, however, from Campania and Tuscany showed that the real offenders were the *officiales*, who had not transferred funds from provincial accounts to the *arca*.

The Emperor thereupon decided that the prefect in office at the time of the deficit should pay: he was dead, therefore his daughters should pay. But they were not the legal heirs of Orfitus and therefore should not be made to shoulder his debts. (It is possible that Orfitus did not make his daughters his heirs because he foresaw the possibility of the matter being opened again.)

Omnes, qui ad amplissimos honorum gradus iudicio clementiae vestrae vel favore provehimur, summo studio debemus eniti, ut famam saeculi suggestionum veritate tueamur, ddd. imppp. quod enim genus gratiae beneficiis principum rependendae fortuna inpar inveniet, si fidem deserat, quae sola munit imperium? 2. contemplanti mihi igitur rescriptum numinis vestri, quo arcae vinariae debita a praefecto eius temporis, quo contracta dicuntur, erui censuistis, silere fas non fuit, quid temporum vestrorum congruat aequitati.

iam primum stupere me fateor caelesti mansuetudini vestrae totius orbis negotiis occupatae *et cui ideo inter multa curarum summatim nonnulla tractanda sunt,*[a] litteras divi Constantii ita esse suggestas, ut comminatio sub condicione deprompta instar cuiusdam debiti duceretur; dehinc tacitum quodam casu de ea parte rescripti, quae tenebat officium, ut persona iudicis tamquam vilior apparitorum suorum inpunitate premeretur; (3) tertio quod ea summa solidorum, quam cognitio et relatio viri inlustris decessoris mei ex maiore parte solutam probavit aerario, tamquam debita et intacta deposcitur. namque XI milia CCCCXLVI solidos ex eo anno, qui Sergii et Nigriniani sequitur consulatum, sacris accessisse thesauris et praefecturae inquisitio et discussorum litterae et v. c. decessoris mei scripta docuerunt.

4. inter haec igitur tam multa valida fidem clementiae vestrae debitam silentio violare non potui, cum vestrum quoque numen adverterem solita cautione neque iudicis

---

[a] *transposed by Seeck*: *after* deposcitur *MSS.* et cui *Seeck:* atque *MSS.*

All of us who are promoted to the most honourable grades of public office by the considered judgement or the favour of your Clemencies, ought to strive with the greatest eagerness to guard the reputation of your era, by keeping to the truth in sending you information, my Lords Emperors. For the inequality of our stations will find no method of returning gratitude for the benefits we receive from emperors if it does not hold fast to the loyalty which alone is the bulwark of the Empire. 2. And so, as I study your Divinities' rescript in which you gave your decision that the debts owed to the treasury of the *arca vinaria* should be exacted from the prefect in power at the time when they are alleged to have been incurred, I felt it was not right for me to forbear from telling you what course of action best befits the equity characteristic of your times.

To begin with, I confess I was dumbfounded that a letter written by the late Constantius should have been represented to your Graces, who are occupied by the affairs of the whole world, and therefore in the multiplicity of your anxieties have to treat some details in a summary way, as carrying the meaning that a threat of penalty made conditionally should be given extended validity just as though it were a debt. Secondly, I was amazed that by some chance nothing was said about that section of the rescript which related to my department, so that the person of the magistrate at its head was attacked as though he was of less importance than the impunity of his own officials. 3. Thirdly, I was amazed that a sum of money in gold is demanded as though still owed, and owed in entirety, when an investigation held by my predecessor, an *illustris*,[2] and his dispatch to the Emperor proved that the greater part of it had been paid to the treasury. For 11,446 gold coins (starting with the year following the consulship of Sergius and Nigrinianus)[3] have been paid in to the sacred depots, and this fact an inquiry at my department, the letter of the auditors, and the written statements of my immediate predecessor, of the distinguished order of senators, have demonstrated.

4. Amid all these valid testimonies I could not be untrue to the loyalty I owe your Clemencies by maintaining silence when I discovered that your Divinities with your usual caution had

---

[2] Sallustius Aventius.   [3] 351.

nomen signasse rescripto et aestimasse, quod conveniendus luce frueretur. nam quando clementia vestra vim veteris comminationis in mortuum tetendisset, cum etiam gravium noxarum poena fine vitae solvatur? at vero iste terror divi principis litteris conprehensus ne viventem quidem posset urgere; gravia enim subiectis saepe minitamini acuendi potius studio quam nocendi. hoc etiam divus genitor tuus in omnium semper animis et ore victurus pia lege constituit, qui sententias quoque sub comminatione depromptas effectu atque exsecutione vacuavit.

5. hanc vero condicionem, quam divus Constantius adiecit litteris suis, multa quae post visa sunt, subruerunt. nam eodem principe adhuc orbem regente ad Tertullum praefectum urbi memorabilem virum migravit exactio, quae si hominis, non potestatis fuisset, circa personam prioris iudicis potuisset[b] haerere; nec multo post tempore inclyti Iuliani Maximum pari honore tunc praeditum tituli istius cura convenit; (6) divo etiam parente numinis tui Romana iura et fata moderante praefectis ac discussoribus *haec* mandata provincia est et per vices administrantium publici debiti cucurrit exactio. novissime relatus in caelum germanus clementiae tuae, cum ipsum Basilium c. v. haberet adpositum, qui personis iudicum non pepercit, primiscrinios urbani officii, quorum sollicitudo per successiones exigenda

[b] oportuisset *Meyer*

not signified in your rescript the name of the magistrate and had assumed that the man to be sued was still alive. Your Clemencies would never have extended the force of an old threat of penalty to make it apply to (*the estate of*) a man already dead, since the penalty imposed on those who have committed even serious crimes is extinguished by death. As a matter of fact, those intimidating words contained in the late Emperor's letter could not worry even a living man; for you often make threats to your subjects with a view to stimulating them rather than hurting them. This idea your late father, who will always live in the minds and on the lips of all men, firmly established when he made a law inspired by his sense of duty; for it was he who cancelled the effect and the execution of sentences passed with a threat of penalty attached to them.[4]

5. Now this condition which Constantius embodied in his letter has been demolished by much that has since become apparent. For, while the same Emperor was ruling the world, the claiming of this money passed to Tertullus,[5] prefect of the city and a man to be remembered; if it had been attached to a man and not to an office, it could have stayed with the person of an earlier holder of the office; again, not much later, in the time of the renowned Julian, charge of the matter fell upon Maximus[6] who at the time was invested with the same office; (6) yet again, when the late Emperor, the father of your Divinity, controlled the rights and the destinies of Rome, this sphere of duty was entrusted to prefects and auditors, and the task of exacting a debt to the state ran on through the changes of administration. And the brother of your Clemency, lately carried off to heaven, since he had at his elbow Basilius,[7] of the distinguished order of senators, a man who did not spare magistrates as individuals, made the chief secretaries of the city department, whose duty it had been, as one prefect succeeded another, to take charge of the assessment of sums to be exacted, actually responsible for the

---

[4] *CTh.* 9. 38. 3, 4.
[5] Tertullus, *praefectus urbi* 359 to 361; see Amm. 17. 11. 5, 19. 10. 1–4, 21. 10. 7.
[6] Valerius Maximus, *praefectus urbi* 361 to January 362. Married St. Melania the Elder. See also Amm. 21. 12. 24.
[7] Basilius, *comes sacrarum largitionum* from 379 to 383; *praefectus urbi* in 395.

curaverat, vel solvendo nomini vel edendae rationi fecit obnoxios.

7. itaque a v. c. ac probatissimo Anicio Basso et Aventio viro spectabili frequentata cognitio et solutam maiorem partem debiti deprehendit et provincialium iudicum repperit sponsionem, qua professi sunt, si urbanum cessaret officium, per se huius tituli integritatem posse sarciri. si igitur haec legibus conferantur, pronuntiabit aeternitas vestra, in professione verum esse nexum, in comminatione terrorem.

quid, quod proxime apparitio cogendis provinciarum iudicibus admota spem debiti eruendi fecisse suggeritur? non est meum famae incerta sectari; inveniet divina maiestas tua, cur huic exactioni perpes cura defuerit.

8. nam socerum meum clarissimae memoriae virum Orfitum petit ista molitio, cuius heredes v. c. et inlustris officiorum magister adscripsit litteris suis, cum tuae mansuetudinis verecundia nullum sacro oraculo nomen expresserit. quid ergo? existimem merito illius factum, qui maior honoribus quam facultatibus ante annos fere quindecim vitam peregit, ut comminatio saepe lecta semper omissa et novis post

balancing of accounts or for the furnishing of a satisfactory explanation.

7. And so a well-attended inquiry held by Anicius Bassus,[8] of the distinguished order of senators and a *spectabilis*, and Aventius,[9] a *spectabilis*, found that the greater part of the debt had been paid, and it discovered too guarantees given by provincial magistrates in which they declared that, if the city office were in difficulties, the total sum under this head could be made good by them.[10] Now, if all this is set beside the (*above-mentioned*) laws for comparison, your Eternities will pronounce that in such a declaration there is a real bond whereas in a threat of penalty there is only intimidation.

And what are we to make of this fact, that recently officials have been engaged in applying pressure to provincial magistrates and are alleged to have furnished hope of raking up the debt? Now it is not for me to pursue uncertainties; your divine Majesty will discover why never-failing care has not been employed in enforcing this demand.

8. The fact is that it is my father-in-law Orfitus,[11] of distinguished memory, whom this intrigue is attacking; it is his heirs, of the distinguished order of senators, whom the *magister officiorum*, of the distinguished order of senators and an *illustris*, cited by name in his letter, though the good feeling of your Graces had named no one in your sacred pronouncement. For about the last fifteen years Orfitus had lived greater in official honours than in fortune; am I then to think that he had done anything to deserve that a threat of penalty, often cited but always left unfulfilled till later it was given interment in new

---

[8] See above, 20 n. 1.   [9] See above, 23 n. 8.

[10] The *arca* received wine from designated areas to sell it at cheap rates to the people. Perhaps the supply of wine had not arrived; the *arca* bought elsewhere; still wine did not arrive and the *arca* would be in arrears; the next governor in whose province the wine-producing area lay would not wish to pay cash instead of wine; the deficit would continue, but the *arca* could claim that credits in its favour lay in the province.

[11] Orfitus. His full name was Memmius Vitrasius Orfitus Honorius; Symmachus married his daughter Rusticiana. Not of aristocratic family, he was the architect of his own *nobilitas*. His career included the offices of *quaestor*, *praetor*, *consul suffectus* (not usually held by the best families), *comes*, proconsul of Africa 352 or 353; he was twice *praefectus urbi*, in 354–6 (Amm. 14. 6. 1) and 357–9 (27. 3. 2). He was exiled and his goods confiscated, but he was reinstated in 367 (27. 7. 3); he died in 370. Cf. Dess. 1243, 3222, 5905.

sepulta decretis, quam neque lex divalis admittit et solutio magnae partis exclusit, resurgat in mortuum, quae non obfuit ante viventi? 9. an meae potius contumeliae causa et ordinem tot ac talium statutorum et divi Gratiani recentem praeceptionem et discussorum diligentiam et praefectorum cognitiones et relationis fidem novis suggestionibus arbitrer sauciari?

testor custodem numinis vestri deum nihil esse, quod iniuria dignus existimer. quieto mihi hanc praefecturam sine ulla adfec*ta*tione tribuistis: si quem forte mordet invidia, si alicuius desideriis rei publicae amore non cessimus, cogitet privata odia adversum leges exercenda non esse; (10) postremo cognoscat, si quis ille est, me meosque successionem clarissimae atque inlustrissimae memoriae viri Orfiti neque ratione iuris neque bonorum aditione cepisse. quaeso igitur, ne in contumeliam iudicii vestri et iuri et innocentiae fraus paretur. quando enim absentibus atque ignorantibus inter alios gesta nocuerunt? quis umquam sententiam numinis vestri inauditus excepit? quando comminatio ad heredes usque porrecta est? certe, ut ipsam causam loquar, quae me ac necessitudines meas vobis propitiis nullo iure contingit, pars maior debiti soluta monstratur, in evidentibus nominibus pars resedit: cuius studio absolvendi sunt debitores, ut inplicentur innoxii?

11. quare insitam divinis sensibus vestris oro iustitiam, ne adversum divi Gratiani definitionem, adversum rescripta tot principum, quae praefectis debita eruenda mandarunt, adversum relationem, quae uberiorem summam docuit exsolutam, reliquum vero secundum rectorum litteras exculpendum ab obnoxiis intimavit, ignaros negotii et paternae hereditatis alienos pulsari incongrua conventione

decrees, allowed by no law of former emperors and precluded by the payment of the greater part of the debt, should be resurrected to apply to a man now dead when it had caused him no embarrassment while alive? 9. Or am I rather to think that to bring me into disgrace is the reason for impugning by new allegations the array of statutes, so numerous and of such character as they are, and the recent directive of the late Gratian and the diligence of auditors and the inquiries of prefects and the truth of dispatches?

I call the god who guards your Divinities to bear witness that there is no reason why I should be thought to deserve harm. I was living in retirement and without any approach by me you bestowed this post of prefect on me. If there is someone whom envy is nagging, if someone to whose longings love of the state has prevented us from yielding, let him reflect that private hatreds ought not to be indulged in defiance of law; (10) and finally let him realize that I and my relatives did not succeed to Orfitus, of distinguished and illustrious family, either by reason of legal right or by entering into property. I ask therefore that no underhand damage should be done to legal rights and innocent parties and so bring your judgement into contempt. When did the acts of one set of people ever inflict injury upon others far removed and unaware of those acts? Who ever received sentence from your Divinities without first being heard? When was threat of penalty extended to cover heirs? Beyond doubt—if I may plead a cause which, if you agree, touches in no point of law either myself or my relations—the greater part of the debt has been shown to have been paid; the remainder lies deposited in accounts available for all to see. In whose interest is it that debtors should be cleared merely to involve other people who are innocent?

11. I appeal therefore to the feeling for justice which is implanted in your divine sensibilities; do not—in defiance of a ruling of the late Gratian, in defiance of all the imperial rescripts which laid the task of investigating debts on prefects, in defiance of the dispatch which explained that the greater part was already paid and reported that the rest, according to letters of governors of provinces, should be prised out of those responsible—do not allow people who know nothing of the matter and who are strangers to the family inheritance to be prosecuted under an

patiaris, neve exemplum novum pius imperator inducas, ut successio *hominum*ᶜ, qui rei publicae profuerant, ad liberos secura non transeat. 12. multos haec forma retinuit et plerosque, ut arbitror, iustius, si qui forte provinciis vestris male abusi sunt; at vero posteritas inlustris memoriae viri Orfiti nihil ex illo aliud quam generis insigne quaesivit. meae tantum iniuriae *studet*ᵈ ista suggestio, nam tenuitati illius frequenter exhaustae nemo testamento, nemo nostrum bonorum aditione successit. unde intellegit clementia vestra, quod non metu familiaris causae, quae legibus tuta est, sed temporum amore solliciter, ne ad innocentiam fisci vestri infructuosa tantum recurrat invidia.

et haec quidem cursim, ne mandatum negotium conperendinatio differret, tantum pro coniugis meae Rusticianae c. f. parte quaesita sunt, cuius germana multo angustior facultatibus ex Etruriae longinquis adesse praecepta est. 13. vestrum vero salutare numen omnes precamur, ne quod de tot provinciis pro maiore parte iam redditum adhuc difficilis exculpat exactio, senatoriae domus inopinata labes speretur posse persolvere. multis nocuit ista condicio, qui rei publicae praefuerunt: neque enim ius si*t*, *ut* una familia novo opprimatur exemplo. quaeso igitur, ut gesta, quae fidem relationis adserunt, audire dignemini legesque percenscatis, quarum plerumque duritiam pro clementia vestra decretis moderatioribus temperastis.

ᶜ *Meyer*: omnium *MSS*.   ᵈ *Meyer*: est ut et *MSS*.

absurd indictment; do not, as a pious emperor, introduce a new precedent by which inheritances left by men who have conferred great benefit on the state shall not pass to their children exempt from interference. 12. The existing rule has restrained many—for the most part and with greater justice those who happen to have ill-treated your provinces; but in fact the descendants of Orfitus, of illustrious memory, have obtained from him nothing but the distinction of belonging to his family. No; it is harm to me that this proposal is aiming at: for to his slender resources so often depleted none of us succeeded by will, and none by entry upon his property. Hence your Clemencies realize that it is not through any fears for the interests of a family, which are protected by the laws, that I am worried, but rather through my love of your era; I do not want malice which will simply bring no profit to anyone to recoil on your unoffending imperial treasury.

These requests are made somewhat hurriedly, for I do not want delay to put off the task laid upon me: they are made solely on behalf of my wife Rusticiana,[12] of the distinguished order of senators; her sister,[13] whose resources are more slender than my wife's, has been instructed to come from the remoter parts of Etruria and to attend here. 13. All of us beseech your Divinities, who can give men safety, not to expect that to inflict an unexpected blow on a senatorial family can produce the money to pay a debt which—though most of it is now paid—it has proved difficult to chisel out of the many provinces concerned. That condition of yours has done harm to many who have been in positions of authority in the state; it would be unjust to set a new precedent and by means of it to ruin one family. I beg you therefore to condescend to give attention to the proceedings which attest the truth of this dispatch and to review the laws, whose harshness with your usual clemency you have often tempered with the greater moderation of your own decrees.

[12] Rusticiana, daughter of Orfitus and wife of Symmachus.
[13] Name not known.

35

This dispatch was sent after **3** and **18**, since the olive-harvest was later than the grain-harvest.

DDD. NNN.

Felicitas quidem vestra indefessas populo Romano copias pollicetur, ddd. imppp., sed cautio iudicum suggerenda non deserit, ut diligentia muniat, quod melior fortuna promittit. frumenti cotidianus usus in facili est; (2) olei tantum species victum plebis tenuiter invecta sollicitat. cuius rei v. c. praefectus annonae, partium suarum diligens executor, praetorianae amplissimae praefecturae, ut ipse adserit, dudum fecit indicium missis de more brevibus, qui angustias patefacerent conditorum. sed ingravescente defectu sileri apud clementiam vestram patriae cura non debuit, cuius spes atque opes bonorum principum favore cumulantur.

3. quare omnes suppliciter oramus, si expectatis preces, qui vota omnium beneficiis praevenitis, ut quam primum iudices Africanos super hac specie Romanis horreis inferenda divinus sermo destimulet. nam properato opus est, priusquam reliquum profliget diurna praebitio. addite igitur hoc munus ceteris, quae praestare consuestis, ut cuncta saeculi bona pari adfluant largitate.

TO OUR LORDS

Your Beatitudes guarantee unfailing supplies for the Roman people, my Lords Emperors; still, cautious magistrates do not neglect, in the proposals they make, to ensure that their vigilance shall safeguard the promises made by better times. No difficulty arises about the daily consumption of corn; (2) oil is the only commodity which owing to meagre imports is threatening the maintenance of the people. The *praefectus annonae* of the distinguished order of senators, who carries out his duties with the greatest care, long ago notified the honourable praetorian prefect, as he himself asserts; he sent summaries,[1] in the usual way, to make clear that the reserves were now very slender. But, as the deficiency became more serious, it would have been wrong for anxiety about our country to be concealed from your Clemencies; it is the graciousness of good emperors that keeps the country's hopes and resources at a high level.

3. Therefore we all beg and supplicate—if indeed you are waiting for prayers when actually you anticipate everyone's desires with your favours—that as soon as possible a divine word from you may spur on the African magistrates in the matter of the import of this commodity to the warehouses of Rome. There is need of haste before the daily issue exhausts what still remains. Add this boon to all the others which it is your practice to grant, so that all the blessings of the times may flow in to us with equal generosity.

[1] *Brevia*. Cf. βρέβιον and examples in LSJ. *CTh*. 10. 6. 3 shows a masculine form. It is common in *CTh.*, but generally in the ablative.

36

Symmachus asks the Emperor not to believe any reports about his slowness in hearing a case delegated to him. There are good reasons for delay.

Dies noctesque sollicitor, ut prompto obsequio divinae clementiae vestrae iussa promoveam; siquidem non licet longa conperendinatione differri iustitiae ac legibus amica decreta, ddd. imppp. unde cauto opus est, ne existimationem meam per alios adlata praeceptis tarditas devenustet. 2. nam cum de Macedonio secus de re publica merito itemque Ammiano dudum mihi iudicium perennitas vestra legaverit, Ammianum quidem protectorum adtestatione cognovi, cum urbis vicina contingeret, languore consumptum; de Macedonio varia iactantur, quem iam pridem debuit custodum sollicitudo perducere. 3. quaeso igitur mansuetudinem vestram, ne mihi fraudi sit mora alieno studio aut torpore contracta, simulque deprecor, ut venerabilis aeternitas vestra singulatim quaerenda distinguat, si forte designatum reum cognitioni meae prosequentium cura tradiderit.

I am worried day and night by anxiety to obey quickly and to carry a step further what your divine Clemencies have ordered me to do: for it is not permitted that decrees so in harmony with justice and the laws should be put off by long delay, my Lords Emperors. So I have to be careful that reports brought by others about slowness in executing commands should not tarnish your good opinion of me. 2. Your Perennities delegated[1] to me some time ago the trial of Macedonius, who had deserved ill of the state, and also of Ammianus; on the testimony of the *protectores* I learnt that when Ammianus[2] reached the outskirts of the city he was done up with weariness; various rumours are flying round about Macedonius[3] whom conscientious guards ought to have produced in person long ago. 3. I therefore ask your Graces not to let delay due to other people's deliberate efforts or laxness count against me; and at the same time I beg that your venerable Eternities will distinguish for me the separate items to be inquired into at the trial—if by any chance the escorts do take the trouble to hand over for my preliminary investigation the man nominated as defendant.

[1] Cf 33.
[2] Apparently a *protector*: Symmachus emphasizes that he tries the case on delegation, for normally the trial of palatine officials would be heard not by him but by their own courts.
[3] Macedonius, *comes sacrarum largitionum* 381; *magister officiorum* 383. After Gratian's death, under whom he was very powerful, he was accused of treason and was sent to be tried before Symmachus (that is, in the court appropriate to senators). He was condemned and apparently put to death.

37

Gratian had cut off supplies of grain from Spain and Alexandria to the *arca frumentaria*. Symmachus complains that not only were supplies deficient for the city's needs, but the *arca* had run into debt. Would the Emperor make a special grant? and restore the old sources of supply?

The debt (§ 2) may be the debt which Auchenius Bassus incurred when prefect and which is mentioned in 23. The dispatch seems to imply that some complaint had been made which incriminated an earlier prefect and officials of the department.

Soli omnium potestis aeternae urbis expensas a defectu sumptuum vindicare, ddd. imppp., maiestati autem vestrae subditae potestates tantum mediocribus causis valent ferre medicinam, magnarum vero rerum mole superantur.

2. ad vos igitur salutaria numina convolamus et opem largam populi Romani inploramus aerario, cum iam diu nihil solitorum vectigalium decretae provinciae contulerunt atque ideo iustus est metus, ne cessantibus subsidiis necessaria deserantur, quae hactenus personae tenues alieno, ut queruntur, aere tolerarunt. super hoc etiam reverendus ordo consultus, cum per se mederi adfectis rebus nequiret, opem vestrae perennitatis oravit. edita ratio est vectigalium, quae Hispaniensis atque Alexandrinus invehere debuit commeatus; expensionum quoque titulos conpetentes officii cura digessit: (3) quaeso, ut omnibus, quae cohaerent, libenter inspectis utilitati publicae velox remedium porrigatis. urgentibus enim causis negari non potest inlatio sollemnis inpendii. quare ferte, ut soletis, propitii auxilium, et qui mentibus piis nova populo Romano beneficia defertis, etiam prisca servate atque urbi vestrae adnuere dignamini, et quod praetermissio praeterita suspendit et quod futurus usus expectat.

You alone are able to rescue the expenditure side of the Eternal City's accounts from being unable to make further payments, my Lords Emperors. The magistrates with powers subordinate to your Majesties can bring relief only to troubles of moderate severity; they are overwhelmed by the sheer size of a big crisis.

2. And so we fly to your Divinities, who restore health to things, and we beg for a generous grant to the treasury of the Roman people. For some time now the provinces appointed for the purpose have contributed nothing of their usual revenues; hence the fear is justified that, if the subventions lapse, ordinary needs will be neglected which up till now low-grade officials of the department have been able to meet only by running up debts, as they complain.[1] Also, the venerable senate was consulted but was unable of its own resources to alleviate the distress and therefore begged the help of your Perennities. A statement has been produced setting out the revenues which the commissariats of Spain and Alexandria[2] should bring in; my conscientious department has summarized the items of expenditure which may be approved. 3. I ask that, when you have examined according to your pleasure all the attached documents, you will extend swift relief to the public interest. The situation is pressing and the usual contribution of funds cannot be refused. Therefore be graciously pleased to furnish aid, as is your habit. Your sense of duty makes you bestow new benefactions on the Roman people; keep up also the old benefactions and deign to grant to your city both what past omissions have withheld from us and also what our future needs look for.

[1] This sentence is taken to mean that officials (*numerarii*) had taken illegal measures to secure grain and had run the department into debt. The subject of *queruntur* is not 'the officials' but individuals lodging the complaint whose names would be given in the attached papers.

[2] Note Alexandria contributing to the corn-supply of Rome.

38

Marcellus complained that he had been violently ejected from his property in Apulia by Venantius, a *strator*. When the case came before the provincial judge, Venantius appealed, on the ground that as a palatine servant his case should have gone to the *vicarius*. With the concurrence of the *vicarius* the judge imposed the usual fine on Venantius for having appealed *a praeiudicio*. The original judge was then to try the charge of *violentia*. But Sallustius Aventius proposed to take the case over himself (as

In negotiis tempore ac iudicatione finitis cessare aequum est longae orationis excursum, ne et numinis vestri salutares actus oneret sermo prolixior et sine argumento rerum loquacitas morosa displiceat, ddd. imppp.

2. cum in iudicio moderatoris Apuli inter Marcellum, qui se deiectum possessione questus est, itemque Venantium stratorem, ut ipse confirmat, eiusque germanam Batrachiam causa violentiae disceptaretur,[a] provocatio a reis inconsulta processit, quod provincialis cognitor promissis litteris ad vicariam potestatem susceptum retineret examen. tunc auditorii sacri iudex rectoris adfatu super appellatione consultus et praeiudicialem multam statuit a provocatoribus[b] inferendam et ipsum quaesitorem crimini dedit cum executione vindictae.

3. post haec obreptionibus partium nonnulla gesta sunt, ut iudicatio consummata traheretur. nam et vir spectabilis decessor meus, cum multam didicisset exactam, quam decreto sacri auditorii appellatio praeiudicialis agnoverat, statuit causam criminis ad se debere transferri, et ego idem secutus partes in examen accivi.

[a] *Seeck*: aedificetur *MSS.*   [b] *Contius*: provocationibus *MSS.*

was permissible to him by his right of *evocatio*): Symmachus inherited it.

Venantius confessed: the case collapsed. The *magister officiorum* had already claimed him, for a *strator* was a palatine under his jurisdiction. Symmachus proposed to hand him over. But it turned out that Venantius was really a member of a town-council, a position which he could not legally renounce. Symmachus could go no further and referred the matter to the Emperor.

When a case has been concluded by time or by final judgement, it is fair that rambling and lengthy talk about it should lapse, so that too luxuriant chatter should not be a nuisance to the beneficent activities of your Divinities, nor an obstinate garrulity unsupported by facts cause your displeasure, my Lords Emperors.

2. A case of violence was argued out in the court of the governor[1] of Apulia between Marcellus, who complained that he had been ejected from his property, and on the other side Venantius, a *strator*, as he alleged, and his sister Batrachia. Without taking advice the defendants launched an appeal, on the ground that the provincial judge, after promising a letter to the Vicar, kept back the case under hearing in his own hands. Then the judge of the sacred tribunal (*the Vicar*), approached and consulted by the governor of the province on the matter of the appeal, ordered that a fine as a penalty for appealing from preliminary proceedings should be paid in by the appellants, and he appointed the original judge to try the case with power of carrying out the penalty.

3. After this, as a result of the manœuvres of the parties, certain things were done to drag out a case already completed. For my immediate predecessor, a *spectabilis*, on learning that the fine which the appeal from the preliminary proceedings had claimed by decree of the sacred tribunal had been demanded, decided that the trying of the charge ought to be transferred to him, and I following the same line summoned the parties for examination.

[1] Apulia and Calabria were under a *corrector*; *moderator* must be a general term: it does not occur as an official title till the time of Justinian.

4. sed cum et tempus reparationis esset emensum, et poenam provocationis aut expectaret aut sumpsisset aerarium, violentiae quoque causam Venantii ac Batrachiae professio ac quorundam capitalis damnatio terminasset, pronuntiavi cognitionem sacri cessare iudicii et Venantium, quem v. c. et inlustris officiorum magister iusserat exhiberi, censui agenti in rebus Decentio, quo prosequente venerat, esse reddendum. 5. sed cum Venantii stratoris inlicitam usurpatamque militiam Marcellus argueret, quod decurionum adscriptus albo, ut gesta docuerunt, adversum leges ad palatina castra transisset, non debui obiecta reticere, ut in ea re, quae modum mei egrediebatur examinis, aeternitas vestra ipsis legibus, quas tuetur, augustior iudicaret.

4. The time for renewal of the proceedings had now gone past; the treasury was either expecting or had already received the penalty for the appeal, when Venantius and Batrachia confessed and certain others were put on a capital charge;[1] that ended the case of violence. I then pronounced that the investigation by the sacred court lapsed, and I ruled that Venantius, whom the *magister officiorum*, of the distinguished order of senators and an *illustris*, had ordered to appear before him, should be handed back to the *agens in rebus*, Decentius, under whose escort he had come. 5. But Marcellus proved that Venantius' post in the imperial service as *strator* was illegal and was falsely claimed; for he had passed into the imperial staff, as the proceedings showed, even though he was enrolled as a member of the council of his town: this was contrary to law.[2] In these circumstances I had no right to keep silence about the facts in front of me; my purpose was that in a matter which went beyond my powers of investigation, your Eternities, who are more august than the very laws you protect, should make the decision.

[1] Agents of Venantius.

[2] The decurions frequently tried to evade their enforced duties and to enter some form of *militia*. Constant legislation tried to prevent it; see e.g. for 384 *CTh.* 12. 1. 94, 95, 100.

39

Till Musa was twenty-five years of age, her affairs and her property had been administered by her *curator*, Acholius, who passed off his brother as Musa's brother and so as co-heir. Reaching the age of twenty-five years she prosecuted Acholius. She was given the usual injunction, which the praetor, who was in charge of the interests of wards, was entitled to give, that her affairs should remain as they were till the case could proceed.

Facit plerumque ratio aut fortuna causarum, ut in controversiis alter aequitate alter iure nitatur; tunc humano labante consilio deliberatio cognitoris ad clementiae vestrae recurrit oraculum, ddd. imppp., quod etiam praesentis negotii qualitas depoposcit.

2. nam Musa annos egressa legitimos, cum in partem rerum paternarum Syntrophium quereretur admissum, quem veluti adultae suae fratrem dolus Acholii curatoris adsciverat, integri restaurationem suffragio iuris accepit, sed multis provocationibus variisque tracta iudiciis intra metas iusti temporis nequivit exequi propositas actiones. 3. ut res monebat, amissum beneficium remedio integravit supplicationis; sed idem mulierem casus etiam rescripti sacri humanitate fraudavit. siquidem mensium quattuor dilata curriculis supremo die temporis impetrati excidit; cognitorem *n*amque successor adveniens praemisso interdicto potestate privaverat. post haec cum vellet infelicem causae lapsum reparatione sarcire, obiectu Constantinianae legis explosa est, quae extra ordinem temporibus indultis longi-

For several reasons she exceeded the statutory four months within which the opening of the case must follow notice of it. A second time she exceeded the time, and then the prefect of the city was succeeded by another: again she was late. Again she appealed for renewal of time. The defendant cited one constitution forbidding renewal: Musa's lawyer quoted another to contradict it. The Emperor was asked to resolve the conflict.

There may be a reason for it, or it may be chance incidental to lawsuits, that often one party to the controversy bases himself on equity, the other on law. When that happens, merely human counsel wavers and the examining judge, as he considers the question, resorts to a pronouncement by your Clemencies, my Lords Emperors; and that is precisely what the nature of the present business asks for.

2. Musa, when she reached legal age, complained that Syntrophius, whom her crafty guardian Acholius had passed off as the brother of his now grown-up ward, had been admitted as heir to part of her father's property. The court supported her and she was awarded restoration of the status quo. But she was held up by many appeals and various judicial proceedings; she was therefore unable to carry through her proposed course of pleading within the limits of the legal period. 3. As the case required, she renewed the claim for her lost inheritance and sought a remedy in supplicating the Emperor; but the same misfortune robbed the poor woman of the kindly consideration of a sacred rescript. Kept waiting for a duration of four months, on the last day of the extension of time she had obtained, she was non-suited, for a successor who arrived to replace the original examining judge had interposed his prohibition and robbed him of any power in the matter. After that when she wished to repair this unfortunate collapse of her case, because the time was exceeded, by getting a renewal of time, the law of Constantine[1] was cited in objection and the case was dismissed; this law refused any further extension if time had already

orem negavit excursum. 4. secuta est provocatio iudicatum. ubi ventum ad sacrae sedis examen et eadem constitutio a Faustino herede Acholii curatoris rursus ingesta est, pars procuratoris, cui actiones Musa mandaverat, non suo vitio causam cecidisse temporibus adprobavit. ad hoc parentum numinis vestri divorum principum protulit sanctionem, quae inter reliquas exceptiones reparationem iurgantibus tribuit, si per cognitorem causa labatur.

5. cum igitur et in Constantiniana lege, qua reparatio adimitur temporibus extra ordinem datis, casus iste cessantis disceptatoris non sit exceptus et recentiora scita divorum cunctis negotiis reparatione subvenerint, si forte a iudice deserantur, facilis in alteram partem esse non potui, sed quod unum remedium convenit rebus ambiguis, fortunam curiosi luctaminis augustissimis legum arbitris reservavi gestis omnibus de more subiectis, ut eorum lectio insinuationis meae adstruat veritatem.

been granted exceptionally. 4. This judgement was followed by appeal. When the matter came before the sacred bench for investigation and the same constitution was again thrust forward by Faustinus, the heir of Acholius her guardian, the other party represented by the agent to whom Musa had entrusted the pleading of her cause proved that it was not their fault that the suit had failed by reason of dates. And, to support his point, he brought forward a decree of your late parents which (among other special cases) assigned litigants the right to renewal of time if a case had exceeded the prescribed period through any fault of the examining judge.[2]

5. And so, in the law of Constantine, which forbids renewal of time if extra time has already been granted exceptionally, the kind of situation I have spoken of, in which a judge fails to sit, is not regarded as an exception, whereas more recent decrees of late emperors have come to the relief of all cases by granting renewal if the judge failed to hear them. So I was not able to be complaisant to either party: but, because only one remedy is suitable when issues are evenly balanced, I have reserved the outcome of this troublesome case to the most august arbiters of the law.

All the proceedings are, as usual, attached, so that a reading of them may support the truth of my statements.

[1] *CTh.* 2. 6. 1 (316).
[2] Valentinian I and Valens. The decree is *CTh.* 11. 31. 2 (365).

40

This dispatch reveals the complicated system of payments and subventions in kind which had grown up among the cities surrounding Rome. They were compelled to supply goods and produce to the capital city and received compensation in various ways; when the balance was upset discontent followed. The chief cities concerned are Tarracina in Latium, and Puteoli on the coast of Campania. A brief summary is as follows:

Tarracina had to provide wood for the *thermae* at Rome and lime for making mortar to repair walls. For this service she received subventions of corn from other cities.

Puteoli was given an annual allowance of 150,000 *modii* of corn from the quantity allocated to Rome. This arrangement held good under Constantine, but Constans halved the allowance. Constantius brought it up to 100,000 *modii*. Capua and other cities also received some of Rome's corn.

In Julian's reign Tarracina complained that it did not get its subvention and therefore could not supply the goods to Rome. The praetorian prefect ordered Puteoli to give Tarracina 5,700 *modii*. Julian was in the East, and so this order never received imperial ratification.

Capua complained that the city prefect Cerealis had cut the grant of corn to herself and other Campanian cities by 38,000 *modii*. Gratian then restored the grant to its old figure.

Puteoli then refused to pay 5,700 *modii* to Tarracina.

Vrbium populorumque luctamina, quoniam sunt maiora privatis, iudicio augustior*i* cedenda sunt, ddd. imppp. merito Puteolanorum ac Tarracinensium causam, quae post Campani moderatoris examen ad sacrum auditorium ex provocatione migravit, cum perspicerem pari lance libratam, maiestatis vestrae arbitrio reservavi. 2. est autem, de quo agitur, eiusmodi:

Puteolanis municipibus divus Constantinus centum quinquaginta milia modiorum in alimoniam civitatis indulsit, quae summa a divo Constante regente rem publicam media parte mutilata est. post Constantius aeque relatus in caelum supplicatione deposita annonam Puteolani populi viginti et quinque milium adiectione cumulavit, atque ita factum est, ut centum milia eiusdem populi victus acciperet. 3. sed divo Iuliano moderante rem publicam, cum Lupus consulari iure Campaniae praesideret *et* Tarracinensium contemplaretur angustias, quod nihil subsidii decreta dudum oppida conferebant, ne commoda populo Romano civitas, quae lavacris publicis ligna et calcem reparandis moenibus subministrat, defectu subito exhausta succumberet, quinque milia et septingentos modios Puteolanis municipibus derogatos Tarracinensium usui deputavit et amplissimae praetorianae sedi statuta et definita suggessit. Mamertinus id temporis praefecturae honore pollebat. is cum disposita

The wrangles of cities and peoples are more important than those of individuals and therefore must be referred to a judgement more august than mine, my Lords Emperors. With good reason therefore I have reserved for your Majesties' decision the case of the peoples of Puteoli and Tarracina which, after being tried by the governor of Campania, was transferred on appeal to the sacred tribunal; for I saw that the issues were very evenly balanced. 2. The dispute is as follows.

The late Emperor Constantine made a grant of 150,000 *modii* of corn to the people of Puteoli for the maintenance of the city; this figure was cut down to a half by the late Constans when he ruled the state. After that, Constantius, now too transported to his place in heaven, in response to an appeal lodged with him raised the supply of corn to the people of Puteoli by 25,000 *modii*, with the result that this people now received 100,000 *modii* for maintenance. 3. But, while the late emperor Julian ruled the state, Lupus,[1] with consular power, was in charge of Campania,[2] and he watched the plight the people of Tarracina were in because the designated towns for a long time had contributed nothing by way of subvention. He was afraid that a city of such service to the Roman people—it provided wood for (*the furnaces of*) the wash-places and lime for repairing the city walls—would be exhausted by any sudden scarcity and would collapse. And so he assigned for the use of the people of Tarracina 5,700 *modii* which had been earmarked for the townsmen of Puteoli, and he proposed to the most noble praetorian department[3] regulations and specifications. At that time Mamertinus[4] held sway as praetorian prefect; he confirmed the arrangements made, but

[1] Virius (?) Lupus, consular governor of Campania 361–3; see *CIL* 10. 3858, 14. 2928.

[2] Originally governed by a *corrector*, but since at least 333 (Dess. 1219) by a *consularis*.

[3] The department of the *praefectus praetorio* in charge of Italy (and Africa, Pannonia, Dacia, and Macedonia), who had general oversight of all the provincial governors in his area.

[4] Claudius Mamertinus, *comes sacrarum largitionum* 361, *praefectus praetorio* of Illyricum and Italy 361–5, consul 362. He was replaced on being found guilty of embezzlement (Amm. 26. 5. 5, 27. 7. 1). Author of speech iii (xi) in *Panegyrici Latini*.

roborasset, nihilominus arbitrium imperiale consuluit neque ullum responsum, quod eo tempore bello Persico rector imperii tenebatur, accepit.

4. exhinc per aliquot annos cucurrit ista praebitio, donec Capuana legatio apud divum atque inclytum Gratianum germanum numinis vestri sua tantum damna deplorans eum frumenti numerum, quem Cerealis ex multis urbibus Romano populo vindicarat, restitui omnibus impetraret. sed occasione rescripti cum sola triginta et octo milia modium, quae horreis aeternae urbis accesserant, provincialium recuperasset alimoniae, etiam quinque milia et septingentos modios Puteolani municipes Tarracinensibus abnuerunt.

5. cum igitur haec causa in iudicium provinciale venisset, v.c. consular*is* non considerata summa, quae rescripto divi principis tenebatur, iudicatione generali omnia Puteolanis reddenda decrevit. verum post appellationem cognitio auditorii sacri, cum illum frumenti modum, qui Campanis fuerat restitutus, a quinque milibus et septingentis modiis, quos ob necessitates urbis aeternae civitas Tarracinensis accepit, *s*ecretum esse perspiceret, manente decreto divalis oraculi ea subsidia, quae Tarracinenses iudicio Lupi et Mamertini praefecti confirmatione capiebant, nec roborare potuit, cum responsi sacri nulla extaret auctoritas, nec demere civitati, ne populus utilitatibus aeternae urbis obnoxius iustis commodis indigeret.

6. ergo ut in rebus dubiis f*i*eri am*a*t,[a] ad clementiae vestrae salubre iudicium convolamus, licet defensio Puteolana post promissam relationem in cassum crediderit provocandum. praesto est gestorum fides, quae perennitatem vestram possit instruere. quaeso atque obsecro, ut negotio multa aetate nutanti tandem stabile remedium deferatur.

[a] *Meyer*: feriam et *MSS*.

all the same he consulted the judgement of the Emperor. He received no reply because the ruler of the Empire was at the moment[5] detained by the war with Persia.

4. For some years the payment ran on until a deputation from Capua, obtaining audience with the late Emperor, your Divinities' distinguished brother Gratian, bewailed its own losses (but only its own) and obtained the answer that the amount of corn which Cerealis[6] had appropriated from many cities for the use of the people of Rome should be restored to all the cities. However, since as a result of the rescript he recovered only 38,000 *modii*—which had (*in the interval*) accrued to the granaries of the Eternal City—for the support of the provincial cities, the townsmen of Puteoli refused to give even 5,700 *modii* to the people of Tarracina.

5. The case went to the provincial court; there the consular, of the distinguished order of senators, disregarding the amount covered by the rescript of the late Emperor, in a general judgement decreed that everything should be paid to the people of Puteoli. But appeal was made and the judge of the sacred tribunal realized that the amount of corn restored to the Campanians was distinct from the 5,700 *modii* which the city of Tarracina received to meet the needs of the Eternal City; the decree, enshrined in a divine pronouncement, still stood, but he was unable to confirm the subvention which the citizens of Tarracina received by the judgement of Lupus endorsed by Mamertinus the prefect, since the authority of a divine reply was not in existence; nor on the other hand could he withhold the sum from the city (*Tarracina*) for fear that its people, which was responsible for supplying the amenities of the Eternal City, should find itself short of the bare necessities of life.

6. And so, as is our habit in these contradictory cases, we fly to your Clemencies' judgement which will put things right, though after we had promised reference to you, defence for the city of Puteoli believed that appeal would be in vain. A faithful account of the proceedings is submitted to you and it will instruct your Majesties. I beg and beseech you that at long last a firm remedy may be applied to a business which over a long period has been in a shaky condition.

[5] In 363.
[6] Naeratius Cerealis, *praefectus annonae* 328 (see *CIL* 6. 1747 for reference to his decision about Campania's contribution); *praefectus urbi* September 352–December 353. See further Amm. 14. 11. 27 and Dess. 731, 5718, 1245.

41

It was open to an informer, who must disclose himself and be ready to appear in court, to notify the *res privata* that a property was without an owner: he might then receive a reward assessed on the value of the property. Aggarea made a will; the heirs entered upon the property; the will was disputed years later on the ground that the testatrix had left a (trifling) honorarium

Certum atque dilucidum est, nihil esse tam familiare legibus quam vestra decreta, ddd. imppp., sed executorum prava interpretatio, dum supplicantibus favet, plerumque iussa corrumpit. statuerat receptus in caelum germanus numinis vestri, cum Marcianus dudum protector Aggareae bona tamquam vacantia postulasset, ut, si ea hereditas scriptum successorem vel legitimum non haberet, in ius fisci tamquam domino nuda concederet; tunc insinuato per rationalem patrimonii modo opperiretur petitor, quid ei sacra deferret humanitas.

2. annus fere secundus est, ut per defensores et rationales augustissimae domus contra iustitiam sollemnis oraculi scripti fatigantur heredes. licet iam sextus annus a testamenti recitatione numeretur, novissime fortuna causae inpetibilem scopulum foedae cognitionis incurrit. nam cum apud virum perfectissimum rationalem Bassianum primo delator bonorum secundum sacra scita p*rod*eretur,[a] novo ausu calcata praescriptio est. 3. dehinc cum testamenti iure confecti fidem recitatio publicaret, calumnia inanis obiecta est, quod signatores nescio quid legati ex eadem voluntate cepissent.

[a] *Seeck*: peteretur *MSS.*

to the witnesses. At a later stage it was urged on behalf of the informer that the *rationalis rei privatae* who had judged the case was acting for the *comes rei privatae*, and therefore the appeal should go to him rather than to the prefect of the city. Symmachus was always chary of running counter to a high official of the palace and so he asks for the Emperor's decision: but he makes it clear that he suspects chicanery and conspiracy.

It is certain and transparently clear that nothing is so akin to the laws as your decrees, my Lords Emperors, but a wrong-headed interpretation of them by those who carry them out often perverts your commands by showing favour to litigants. Your Divinities' brother now received into heaven had given his decision when Marcianus, in former time a *protector*, asked for the property of Aggarea as being property without an owner; he had ordered that, if the inheritance had no heir nominated in the will and no legitimate successor, it should pass, as lacking an owner, into the jurisdiction of the fisc; then, when the *rationalis* had provided information about the extent of the estate, the suppliant should wait to see what the Emperor in his humanity would grant him.

2. For nearly two years the nominated heirs have been pestered by barristers and *rationales* of the most august palace in defiance of the justice of an imperial pronouncement. It is now six years since the reading of the will, and quite recently the case has run into an intolerable snag presented by a disgraceful preliminary court of inquiry held before the *rationalis* Bassianus, of *perfectissimus* rank. First of all the man who had informed about the property was produced, as the sacred ordinances require,[1] but by a novel piece of audacity objection made to this was stamped down. 3. Next, though the reading of the will made public the validity of a will legally completed, a malicious charge, quite groundless, was brought up, that the witnesses had

[1] *CTh.* 10. 10. 8, 9, 12.

adduntur etiam rescripta divalia, quibus adstipulatio cuiusdam remota est, qui suam iuvisse causam testimonio diceretur, quasi vero simile esset exemplum aut tenuis honor, quo
subscriptores ob amicitiam defunctus adsperserat, legitimum
posset abolere iudicium. nam si his legibus viveremus,
inimicis signatoribus tutius uteremur, quorum offensa nihil
de testatore humanitatis exigeret.

4. piget dicere in quinque numero solidis potissimum sub-
scriptoris fuisse legatum; ceteris enim magis commemoratio
honesta quam pecuniae quaestus accessit. ergo aut ex-
tremae paupertatis successio fuit, si putatur exiguus honor
fidem legitimi iudicii sauciasse, aut si census hereditarius
existimatur uberior, aliena est a suspicionibus brevis summa
legati. quis non familiarissimum quemque signandis adhibet,
cum extrema conduntur? iam quid mirum est, si in oculis
positus mereatur aliquod monumentum religionis, qui meruit
advocari? 5. non fero signatorem, cui pars bonorum magna
defertur, nam etsi integra conscientia non tamen sincero
pudore ditatur; at vero haec levia pignora aut amoris gratia
aut testatoris verecundia relinquuntur. nihil huic religioni
novis legibus derogatum est; manet iste usus et vobis iura
servantibus semper manebit: unus et solus post humani
generis[b] memoriam rationalis emersit, qui exemplum novae
iudicationis induceret.

6. hinc orta est provocatio, quae ubi auditorium sacrum
decreto etiam vestrae legis intravit, rursus eludendi iudicii
causa propositum est inane commentum, ut ab inlustri viro
privatae rei comite delegata cognitio diceretur rationalis

[b] *inserted by Seeck*

received something by way of legacy under this same expression of wishes. And imperial rescripts were also quoted under which the assent of a person is barred who is alleged to have benefited by bearing witness[2]—as if indeed this were a parallel instance or as if a trifling honorarium, which the deceased had bequeathed in the name of friendship to those who subscribed their signatures as witnesses, could possibly annul a will declared legal. If this were the kind of laws we were living under, it would be safer for us to use our enemies as witnesses, on the ground that animosity would look for no kindly feelings on the part of the testator.

4. I am disgusted to tell you that the witness's legacy was at most five *solidi*; the rest were awarded rather an honourable mention than any monetary gain. And so, either the estate for disposal to the heirs was extremely exiguous, if a minute honorarium is considered to have damaged the validity of a legal judgement, or else, if the value of the inheritance is deemed fairly substantial, a slight sum by way of legacy is removed from suspicion of any kind. Naturally everyone employs his closest friends for signing documents when his last dispositions are being made. It is not at all surprising that a man who is thought worthy to be called in as witness should be openly acknowledged as worthy of some token of the testator's feeling of obligation to him. 5. I cannot tolerate the witness to a will who receives a good proportion of the property; he becomes richer perhaps with a clear conscience but not with a real sense of decency; but these trifling tokens are bequeathed to signify the affection or the respect of the testator. No new laws derogate in any way from this sense of obligation; the practice of expressing it remains, and as long as you preserve what is right, it always will remain. The one and only person within human memory to introduce a sample of new adjudication was an upstart of a *rationalis*.

6. This was the origin of the appeal. By the fiat of your law it came before the sacred tribunal; again the attempt was made to elude judgement by the introduction of a worthless fabrication, which urged that the preliminary investigation had been delegated by the *comes* of the *res privata* to the *rationalis* for his inquiry

---

[2] Perhaps *CTh*. 2. 2 covers the point, cf. also *Dig*. 22. 5. 10 (Pomponius). But *Dig*. 28. 1. 20 seems to allow a legatee to benefit. English law accepts the testimony as valid but refuses the legacy.

examini atque ideo rursus ad eiusdem iudicium debere transferri, cum omnis quaestio ex precibus Marciani dudum protectoris et vestrae clementiae largitate descendens sacro potius auditorio ex provocatione conpeteret, accedente etiam proxima sanctione, quae indiscrete huiusmodi appellationes sedi, quae vicem principum tuetur, prisco iure commisit.

7. examinatis igitur omnibus pronuntiavi bona obnoxia non esse rescripto, cum vestri numinis aeterna iustitia, si scriptis aut legitimis successoribus vacaret hereditas, fiscum statuisset admitti, has autem facultates Marcellus Bizias et Heliodorus iusta defuncti voluntate cepissent. tunc sententiam meam defensor venerabilis domus inusitata provocatione suspendit. 8. sed cum huius rei nullum exemplum cognitionalis extare suggereret, nihilo minus obiectam vocem libenter admisi et relatione summatim cuncta conplexus gestorum quoque documenta subtexui, praesumens bonis placitura principibus, quae secundum leges pro fama temporum iudicavi.

and that therefore it ought to be transferred back to his court. And this in spite of the fact that the whole question, which came down from the petition presented by Marcianus, a former *protector*, and from the gift made to him by your Clemencies, fell within the competence rather of the sacred tribunal[3] because it was on appeal; besides this there was the recent ruling[4] which, without making any distinctions, committed, by long-established law, appeals of this kind to the bench which represented the Emperors.[5]

7. And so I examined all the parties and gave as my judgement that the property was not affected by the rescript,[6] since your Divinities' eternal justice decided that the fisc should be given entry to a property only if there were no nominated or legitimate heirs to it; but in fact Marcellus, Bizias, and Heliodorus had taken over the property by virtue of the validly expressed wishes of the deceased. At that point the barrister of your venerable palace suspended proceedings by lodging an unprecedented appeal. 8. Now, though the *cognitionalis* stated that there was no precedent for such an appeal, I was glad all the same to allow the objection, and in this dispatch I have summarized all the points and have attached the minutes of the proceedings, for I take it for granted that good Emperors will be pleased by the judgement I have given, which is in accordance with law and has regard for the good name of the times.

[3] Symmachus' own court.   [4] *CTh.* 11. 30. 41.
[5] The appellate courts of the *praefectus praetorio*, the *praefectus urbi*, and *vicarii* were regarded as imperial courts acting for the Emperor.
[6] Conferring a conditional grant of the property on Marcianus.

42

Asks that a certificate of good service should be granted to a *cornicularius*.

Petronianus urbanarum dudum cohortium miles ad corniculorum gradum inculpati laboris diuturnitate provectus more institutoque maiorum testimonium meruit castrensis industriae, quod ceteris quoque post honestum cursum stipendiorum iudicia detulerunt, ddd. imppp. Valentiniane Theodosi et Arcadi inclyti victores ac triumphatores semper Augusti. dignum est igitur divina temporum vestrorum felicitate, ut peractam sine offensione militiam, si perennitatis vestrae pius vultus adriserit, praerogativa sollemnis exornet.

Petronianus, who served for a long time in the city cohorts[1] and was promoted to the rank of *cornicularius* after long and blameless work has earned, according to established custom and tradition, the certificate testifying to his diligence in the service,[2] which imperial decisions have awarded also to others after an honourable career, my Lords Emperors Valentinian, Theodosius, and Arcadius, renowned conquerors and winners of triumphs, for ever Augusti. It would accord, then, with the divine felicity of your times that the usual privilege, if your Perennities' divine countenances would smile upon the proposal, should crown service which has been performed faultlessly.

[1] That is, before the urban cohorts were converted into civil servants serving in government departments, especially the *officium urbanum*, see s.v. in Glossary.

[2] He wanted the certificate for further employment, perhaps as *agens in rebus*.

43

Symmachus agrees that the senate's resolution to erect equestrian statues of Theodosius the Elder should be communicated to Theodosius and Arcadius; see also **9**.

Curae mihi est, ut qui animis et maiestate congruitis, mutua honorificentia gaudeatis. dignum est igitur, domine imperator Valentiniane inclyte victor ac triumphator semper Auguste, ut decretum senatus ad invictissimos fratres numinis tui, si ita placet, clementia tua insinuante perveniat. 2. quorum auctor et parens, ut dudum v. c. et inlustri officiorum magistro scripsisse memini, statuarum equestrium honore decoratus est, quas ei ordo venerabilis Africani et Brittannici belli recordatione decrevit ea scilicet causa, ut iustis superiorum ducum titulis praesentium circa vos devotio provocetur.

I am anxious that you who are so alike in mind and in dignity should find a common pleasure in the honours we offer you. It is right therefore, my Lord Emperor Valentinian, renowned conqueror and winner of triumphs, for ever Augustus, that, as your Clemency suggested, the decree[1] of the Senate should be conveyed, if it please you, to the unconquered brothers[2] of your Divinity. 2. Their author and father, as I recollect writing some time ago to the *magister officiorum*, of the distinguished order of senators and an *illustris*, was given the distinction of equestrian statues of himself;[3] our venerable order decreed them as a memorial of the wars in Africa and in Britain; their intention was that the well-deserved inscriptions celebrating leaders of earlier times should stimulate the present generation to be loyal to you.

[1] Loosely for *senatus consultum*.
[2] Not strictly used. [3] See above, 9 n. 2.

44

The *mancipes salinarum*, who contracted for the working of the salt-pans at Ostia and paid an annual sum for the right, found themselves so depleted in number by irregular exemptions that they were impoverished and could not undertake the responsibilities of their guild. The *navicularii*, shippers, originally sixty in number, were required as a guild to transport wood from specified districts to supply the furnaces of the baths at Rome. The *mancipes* asked that the *navicularii* should share the work; they however refused that their guild should be so committed but were willing to surrender a few of their members. Symmachus asks for imperial approval.

This dispatch shows (i) that the guilds worked out arrangements between themselves and then obtained the authority of rescripts, of which *CTh*. contains very many examples, (ii) that many illegally obtained rescripts granted by palatine servants often endangered the smooth working of the administration.

Cum mancipes salinarum magno ex numero ad paucos redacti necessitatis publicae molem ferre non possent, delata supplicatione meruerunt, ut his ......[a] qui ante *s*ecreti atque excusati fuerant, redderentur et ex aliis corporibus seu vacantibus iusta supplementa incunctanter acciperent, ddd. imppp. allegata igitur praeceptione divina, cum plerosque consortio suo ante *s*ecretos muniri Macedonii suffragio repperissent, relationem super eorum muniminibus impetrarunt. vestrae tantum clementiae liberum est inique elicita rescripta rescindere. 2. tunc urgente defectu navicularios aeque lignorum obnoxios functioni ad parem sollicitudinem vocare coeperunt, ut utriusque corporis cura coniuncta indiscretum munus agnosceret. at illi nonnullos de turmalibus[b] suis tradere maluerunt quam in societatem tanti oneris convenire. itaque factum est, ut volentibus iisdem certi homines ma*n*cipibus iungerentur.

nunc perennitatis vestrae stabilem censionem publica causa deposcit, ne obreptivis supplicationibus subsidia integrati corporis subruantur. 3. relationi gesta coniunxi tam de *i*is habita, quos Macedonii interventus absolverat, quam me disceptante confecta, quibus sine vexatione cuiusquam voluntas naviculariorum nonnullos ma*n*cipibus deputavit. erit iam sacrosancti numinis vestri et illorum antiquare suffragia, quos ostenditur ambitus liberasse, et his obstruere aditum supplicandi, quos sui corporis adiudicavit adsensus.

[a] obsequiis *Seeck*   [b] *Seeck suggests* de decurialibus

The contractors of the salt-pans, whose large number has been reduced to very few, were not able to bear the burden of the vital public service they perform; they were justified in supplicating you, asking that all their members who had been seconded and exempted should be returned to perform these services and that they should immediately receive reinforcements from other guilds and from titular members, my Lords Emperors. A divine directive was quoted; the contractors found that most of the men formerly seconded were protected by the support of Macedonius,[1] and therefore they asked and were granted that the question of their protection should be referred back. But only your Clemencies are free to cancel rescripts unfairly extracted (*from the Emperor*). 2. Then, as the shortage became pressing, they began to summon the guild of *navicularii*, who were equally liable to serve as transporters of logs, to take an equal share of responsibility, so that each guild should combine with the other and recognize that their service was undivided. But they preferred to hand over a few of their members rather than enter into such a burdensome partnership. Thus it came about that with the concurrence of the guild certain individuals were assigned to the contractors.

The public interest now demands that a firm expression of your views should be made by your Perennities, to prevent backdoor supplications from undermining the resources of a guild now brought up to establishment. 3. I have attached to this dispatch the proceedings relating to the men released by Macedonius' intervention and an account of the measures decided on in my court; as a result of them the goodwill of the *navicularii* assigned a few of their number to the contractors and did no one any harm. It is now the task of your sacred Divinity to cancel the support given to the men whom it is obvious that private intrigues exempted, and to deny a hearing to any supplications by men whom the general wish of their own guild assigned as it did.

[1] See above, 36 n. 3.

45

This dispatch is a covering letter sent with a return of newly elected magistrates—quaestors, praetors, and *consules suffecti*. Since the election took place in the senate on 9 January, this dispatch must be dated after that day in 385.

As head of the senate Symmachus was the channel of communication between Emperor and senate. Senatorial rank was of great importance, partly as a matter of prestige, partly for the exemption which it carried (especially from the duty to serve as *decurio*), though these exemptions were offset by special taxes and levies (**46,** n. 1).

Devotione et more commonitus magistratuum nomina, quibus varias functiones designationum tempore amplissimus ordo mandavit, ad aeternitatis vestrae perfero notionem, ut muneribus exhibendis aut subeundis fascibus destinatos cognitio imperialis accipiat. his copulati sunt, quos senatui vestro recens ortus adiecit. prolixus in talibus rebus esse non debeo, cum decreti publici fides gestorum potius insinuationem postulet quam largum referentis eloquium.

Entry to the senate was open to sons of senators who had held the praetorship. But the Emperor also appointed to the senate: he granted *codicilli* which conferred the rank of *clarissimus*. The recipient then became a member of the order; he informed the prefect of the grant who put the matter to the senate which then voted—no doubt in favour. (The procedure we know from Symmachus himself, see e.g. *Or.* 6, 7, 8; *Ep.* 7. 96, 9. 118.) Or the Emperor could appoint a man to a post which by custom carried senatorial rank, and so he could enlarge the senate with high imperial officials.

A record of the property of senators was kept by the *censuales*; in 46 Symmachus reported the latest figures and recent changes. These figures provided the basis of taxation and levies.

Loyalty and tradition lead me to bring to the notice of your Eternities the names of the magistrates to whom the noble order assigned their varied duties at the time of the appointments, so that imperial scrutiny may approve the men who are marked down to provide shows for the city and to bear the insignia of office. Attached to this list are the names which recent births have added to your senate. In such matters I must not be diffuse; a public decree, to be true to the facts, demands a plain statement of what was done rather than the ample rhetoric of the informant.

46

Another covering letter, supplementary to 45.

Etiamsi prisca institutio mittendis ad clementiam vestram censuum brevibus cursum vel ordinem[a] non dedisset, ddd. imppp. Valentiniane Theodosi et Arcadi inclyti victores ac triumphatores semper Augusti, diligentia tamen boni saeculi fidem publicae instructionis exigeret. siquidem convenit principes et parentes humani generis edoceri, quid reverendo ordini vel senatorum novorum accessus adiciat vel glebae excusationibus detrahatur. 2. harum rerum aeternitati vestrae fidum exhibebit indicium trimestris instructio, quam sollemniter sumptam de officio censuali paginis relationis adnexui, ut maiestas vestra cognoscat, qui in amplissimam curiam collegarum numerus influxerit, et quid censibus senatoriis aut novi professio incrementi dederit aut exemptio veteris amputarit.

[a] *Seeck suggests* cursum sollemnem

Even if past rules did not prescribe any course or order for the submission of summaries of census-ratings to your Clemencies, my Lords Emperors Valentinian, Theodosius, and Arcadius, renowned conquerors and winners of triumphs, for ever Augusti, still the attention to detail suitable to a good era would demand exact truth in a return supplied to the state. For it is fitting that the princes and fathers of the human race should be thoroughly acquainted with recent accessions of new senators to the venerable order, and with losses to the revenue caused by exemptions from the senatorial surtax on property.[1] 2. The three-monthly return, which as usual I have extracted from the census office and attach to the pages of my dispatch, will give a faithful picture of these matters to your Eternities. Thus your Majesties will learn how many (*new*) colleagues have entered the most noble senate, and what additions have been made to senatorial assessments by declarations of enlargement of property, and what diminutions caused in the old figures by loss of property.

[1] Instituted by Constantine, the *collatio glebalis* was an annual tax levied at a graduated rate on land owned by senators and collected by the *censuales*. Exemptions were rare.

47

A letter congratulating the Emperors on recent victories.

Bellorum quidem vestrorum gloriosos exitus fama non occulit, sed maior est victoriae fides, quae oculis adprobatur, ddd. imppp. Valentiniane Theodosi et Arcadi inclyti victores ac triumphatores semper Augusti. dudum fando acceperat Romanus populus caesorum funera Sarmatarum, at nunc confirmata est nuntiorum laetitia spectaculo triumphali. iam minores non sumus vetustatis exemplis: vidimus, quae *lecta* mira*ba*mur, catenatum agmen victae gentis induci illosque *tam truces* pridem vultus misero pallore mutatos. stetit harenae medio subiecta voluptati, quae fuit ante formidini, et adsuetae armis gentilibus manus gladiatoria instrumenta timuerunt.

2. felicem nimis belli istius ducem, qui divinae clementiae vestrae fretus auspiciis ex hostium numero alios ad securitatem provinciarum penitus extinxit, alios ad laetitiam plebis Martiae reservavit. merito illi iudicia vestra respondent, iure in litteris imperialibus saepe celebratur; neque enim tanta devotio digniorem possit invenire praeconem. sit vobis frequens usus ac facilis laurearum, et eos, qui forte ausus inpios in Romanum nomen extulerint, fortitudo militum capiat, harena urbis expendat. perpetua haec devotis civibus virtutis vestrae tamquam tributa praestetis.

Rumour does not conceal the splendid outcome of your wars, but a victory gains greater credence if it is confirmed by sight, my Lords Emperors Valentinian, Theodosius, and Arcadius, renowned conquerors and winners of triumphs, for ever Augusti. Some time ago the Roman people had received verbal reports of the deaths of the slaughtered Sarmatians, but now the glad news has been corroborated by a triumphal spectacle. We do not now fall short of the precedents set by antiquity; we have now seen things which surprised us when they were read out to us— a column of chained prisoners from a conquered race led in procession, and faces once so fierce now changed to a pitiable pallor. A race which once was terrifying to us stood in the middle of the arena, now the object of our delight, and hands trained to wield outlandish weapons were afraid to meet the equipment of gladiators.

2. Happy indeed was the general[1] in that war who relied on the auspices of your divine Clemencies; out of the total number of the enemy, some he utterly annihilated to safeguard the provinces, others he kept to amuse the people of Mars. You were right in your judgement when you sent him a dispatch, and with reason he is often celebrated in your imperial letters; for indeed such loyalty as his could find no one more worthy to blaze abroad his fame than yourselves. May you enjoy the laurels of victory often and easily; as for those who from time to time venture upon wicked attacks against the name of Rome, let our brave soldiers take them prisoner and let the arena in the city finish them off. And for your devoted citizens may you ever provide what we may call tribute to your own high qualities.

[1] This victory must have occurred recently, perhaps in 383, and by an army of Theodosius. It is not known what general is meant. For other captives see **9**.

48

The question at issue is a point of procedure; are *clarissimi* living in the provinces to be tried on a civil charge by the ordinary courts appropriate to the case or do special rules apply to them? The legal position of *clarissimi* had been bitterly contested for years and had varied from time to time (cf. 31), and from this dispatch it seems that in some respects it was still in doubt.

Catulus, a *clarissimus* living in a province, had left property: *clarissimi* inherited and had long been in possession. The *res privata* made a claim on the estate. The case came before Gratian:

Certa officia sunt omnium potestatum: praefecturae urbanae proprium negotium est senatorum iura tutari, ddd. imppp. quare partium mearum conventus necessitate allegationibus clarissimorum virorum iusta poscentium deesse non potui.

a quibus pleraque servitia palatinus Eusebius iussus eruere, ut bonorum Catuli clarissimae memoriae viri quaestio iudicationibus sacrisque responsis consumpta repetatur, optimatium querimonias, qui dudum partis fruuntur, excivit. 2. ventum est igitur ad leges executore cupiente .... [a] quem contradictio repellebat, inplorataeque vestri numinis sanctiones, quae senatorum controversias transferri ab urbano foro ad peregrina vetuerunt.

sed cum adsererem, non eandem praerogativam esse ...... [b] servorum, quibus supplicantibus certum perennitas

---

[a] ut causa ad cognitionem v.c. et inlustris comitis rerum privatarum ex sacro rescripto transferretur *Seeck*   [b] in causa *Seeck*

the *clarissimi* persevered. Some slaves of Catulus now put in a complaint direct to the Emperor. The question was whether the slaves should be heard in a provincial court—and so the competence of the *praefectus urbi* was challenged—or whether, since the property of *clarissimi* was concerned, the case belonged to the prefect. They therefore petition the Emperor through Symmachus to resolve the conflict of rescripts; in the opening sentence Symmachus states the matter as one of general importance.

All magistracies have clearly defined duties; the business peculiar to the prefecture of the city is to safeguard the rights of senators, my Lords Emperors. That is why, compelled to take action by the duties of my role, I could not fail to listen to the statements of distinguished members of the senatorial order when they made very just demands.

The palatine official Eusebius had been ordered to make these senators surrender a number of slaves so that the inquiry into the property left by Catulus, of distinguished memory, which was taken up with judicial procedures and sacred replies, might be resumed. This prospect excited the protests of members of the noble families who have long been enjoying what they had got (*under the will*). 2. And so at last the matter came to the test of the laws themselves: the court's officer wanted the case transferred, as a sacred rescript directed, to the court of the *comes* of the *res privata*, of the distinguished order of senators and an *illustris*. He was repulsed by the lodging of a formal objection, and the enactments of your Divinities were invoked which said that disputes involving senators should not be transferred from a city court to a court outside Rome.[1]

I maintained that this special provision did not apply in the case of slaves who had supplicated the Emperor and for whom your Perennities had appointed a particular examining judge; the answer made to me was that the request to have the case

[1] This refers to the rule *actor rei forum sequitur*, and to *domicilium dignitatis* by which the home of a senator abroad is regarded as being at Rome.

vestra detulit cognitorem, responsum est, quod fortunas clarissimarum personarum precatio subtilis incesserit.

3. inter haec cum Donatus adsisteret ceteris precatoribus sacro iunctus oraculo, quaesivi, ut mos est, ne eodem nomine alius subderetur, quae hominem condicio haberet et an ipse de Catuli iudicio supplicasset. tunc ille Hilariani clarissimi viri servum professus ab illarum precum conscientia, quas dicitur obtulisse cum ceteris, alienum se constanter adseruit; atque ita visa est supplicationis fides etiam de auctore nutare.

4. adiecta sunt alia plena iuris atque rationis, quod post crebras cognitiones et rescripta ad relationem numerosa poenam legis inciderint, qui denuo contra vetitum supplicarunt. extant quippe sententiae, quas cum provocatio temptasset inhibere, consultus relatione divus genitor clementiae vestrae finem posuit quaestioni. cui victoriae fiscus accessit emolumentum bonorum Catuli clarissimae memoriae viri, ut adsertum est, pro certa parte sortitus.

5. cum igitur senatorum allegatio rescriptis ac legibus niteretur, maluerunt causam suam vestrae per me aperire iustitiae quam legitimo vindicare iudicio, securi decretorum, quae et necessitate iuris et divi patris veneratione servabitis. itaque servos bona fiducia tradiderunt; quos in praeiudicium absentium post consummationem negotii aequitas temporum, quantum praesumimus, non patietur audiri.

transferred was an underhand attack on the fortunes of persons of distinguished rank.

3. Meanwhile Donatus was present in court, being associated with the rest of the suppliants by command of a sacred pronouncement; following usual practice I asked him—for I did not want anyone else of the same name to be substituted—what his status was and whether he himself had supplicated the Emperor in the matter of the lawsuit against Catulus. He stated he was the slave of Hilarianus, of the distinguished order of senators, and he firmly declared that he had no knowledge whatever of the petition which he is alleged to have made together with the rest. And so the trustworthiness of the supplication was clearly somewhat shaky, even with regard to the identity of its author.

4. Other additional points were raised, full of law and reasoned argument—how, after frequent hearings and numerous rescripts in reply to references to the Emperor, people who in spite of being prohibited appealed all over again met the penalty of the law. There are on record, you see, certain legal judgements; when an appeal tried to stay them, your Clemencies' late father, reference being made to him, put an end to the whole inquiry. So victory was won and the fisc joined in, having obtained, so it was said, a fixed proportion of the assets in the estate of Catulus, of distinguished memory.

5. Since, then, the senators' depositions rested on rescripts and enactments, they preferred to lay their case through me before your sense of justice rather than to justify it in the proper court; they felt secure in the decrees which you will maintain; for you will be influenced both by the requirements of the law and by respect for your late father. And so in all confidence they handed over the slaves; the justice of the times, we take for granted, will not permit them, after the business has been fully settled, to be heard with possible prejudice to absent parties.

49

Symmachus asks for indulgence to a young and imprudent civil servant.

Quid habeat condicionis inscriptio, prae ceteris nostis iuris publici conditores, ddd. imppp. Valentiniane Theodosi et Arcadi inclyti victores ac triumphatores semper Augusti.

provisum est enim, ne quis temere in alieni capitis discrimen irrueret, ut se *eius*dem[a] prius poenae sponsione vinciret. 2. secundum haec scita legum agens in rebus Africanus accusationem professus Campano et Hygino clarissimis viris violentiae crimen obiecit. continuo, ut severitas exigebat, reos custodia militaris dissimulata dignitatis *reverentia*[b] circumdedit;

sed ubi partes sub examine constiterunt, multo luctamine patronorum decursa cognitio oratione magis quam probationibus redundavit. 3. cum longa verborum serie causa traheretur, summates Aricinae urbis, quos ut conscios accusator exciverat, adhibuimus quaestioni, gestorum ordinem sciscitamur: omnium convenit adsertio, nihil turbarum esse conflatum. tunc ad eludendum iudicium praesentia cuiusdam coepit exposci, quem non tenebat inscriptio. eo denique res rediit, ut a partibus Africani accusationis omissio desperatione peteretur.

supererat ut crimine non probato in accusatorem formidata reis poena transiret; (4) sed cum me Africani militia pariter atque incauta adolescentia permoveret, malui iudicium de eo clementibus reservare. alia est enim condicio

[a] *Seeck*: idem *MSS.*   [b] *inserted by Seeck*

The conditions which attach to an indictment you know better than the rest of us, for you establish the public system of law, my Lords Emperors Valentinian, Theodosius, and Arcadius, renowned conquerors, winners of triumphs, for ever Augusti.

To prevent anyone rushing ill-advisedly into an action involving the personal rights of another man, it has been provided that a plaintiff shall bind himself by giving a prior undertaking to undergo the same penalty (*if he should lose*).[1] 2. Accepting these regulations Africanus, an *agens in rebus*, gave notice of indictment and brought a charge of violence against Campanus and Hyginus, both of the distinguished order of senators. Immediately, as strict procedure demanded, a military guard surrounded the defendants, deference to their rank being thus disregarded.

When the parties stood in court under examination, the preliminary proceedings ran on amid much wrangling on the part of the barristers on each side and was prolific rather of rhetoric than of proofs. 3. The case dragged on with a trail of verbiage until I summoned to the investigation the chief men of the city of Aricia,[2] whom the plaintiff had called as having knowledge relevant to the charge. I ascertained the order of events: everybody's statement agreed that no disturbance had been created. Thereupon, with the intention of misleading the court, a demand was made for a certain person to attend to whom the charge did not relate. And so the matter came back in the end to a request made by the plaintiff's side in sheer desperation that the indictment should be allowed to drop.

It only remained then, since the charge was not proved, that the penalty with which the defendants had been threatened should be transferred to the plaintiff. 4. But Africanus was a member of the civil service, and he was young with the heedlessness of youth; these considerations influenced me equally and I preferred to leave judgement on him to merciful judges.

[1] *CTh.* 1. 5, 8, 9, 11, 14.
[2] In Latium on the *Via Latina*.

magistratuum, quorum corruptae videntur esse sententiae, si sint legibus mitiores, alia est divinorum principum potestas, quos decet acrimoniam severi iuris inflectere. relationi gesta subtexui, partium quoque subplementa sociavi. quaeso augustissimam perennitatem vestram, ut perpensis omnibus sequenda iubeatis.

Magistrates and emperors are in different situations: magistrates' sentences are thought to be corrupt if they are milder than those which the laws prescribe, whereas it is becoming to the authority of divine emperors to bend the severity of strict law. I have attached the proceedings to my dispatch, and to these I have added the supplementary statements made by the parties. I ask your most august Perennities to weigh all these matters and to instruct me as to the course I should follow.

ADDITIONAL NOTES

15. Lydus (time of Justinian) preserved the tradition 'they gave presents of daphne which they called strena to do honour to some divinity with this name, who was the guardian of victories' (*de mensibus* 4. 4). Augustine, too, knew of Strenia ('Strenia dea sit strenuum faciendo', *C.D.* 4. 11) and of the celebration of the *strenae* on January 1 ('acturus es celebrationem strenarum sicut paganus, lusurus alea et inebriaturus te', *Serm.* 198. 2, on the Kalends of January). Shrubs with strongly scented leaves were supposed to have a purifying effect; the New Year was to start purified from the bad omens of the previous year. In a triumphal procession soldiers wore laurel to cleanse them from blood, cf. Paulus–Festus 117 M: 'laureati milites sequebantur currum triumphantis ut quasi purgati a caede humana intrarent urbem. Itaque eandem laurum omnibus suffitionibus adhiberi solitum erat, vel quod medicamento siccissima erat vel quod omni tempore viret ut similiter respublica floreat'.

The goddess Strenia then is a deification of the purifying powers of certain shrubs—laurel according to Lydus, vervain according to Symmachus; vervain was much used in medicine. Symmachus alone attributes the origin of the custom to Tatius. Lydus says the word *strena* was Sabine; Tatius was a Sabine king.

19. The following note amplifies the introductory summary.

Gaudentius denied the validity of Liberius' mandate which had applied to Principius, now dead. This point Sallustius Aventius referred back to the praetor, who said it was valid. Gaudentius tried the same plea before Symmachus, who also maintained the validity. Gaudentius said the validity lapsed with the death of Marciana senior; Symmachus cited *CTh.* 11. 12. 1 to prove that it did not lapse. Gaudentius then delayed the valuation of the properties inherited; Liberius wanted such valuation in order to make his case and asked Symmachus to authorize a *missio in possessionem* with a view to safeguarding the properties. Gaudentius halted this by finding a flaw (*praescriptio mendaciorum*) in the *supplicatio*; he said that Liberius quoted *all* the daughters

of Placidianus as heirs in Prisca's will, but in fact the name of Marciana junior was not contained in it; it was not obvious therefore why she was being attacked. Liberius replied that it was because she was already in possession of the properties which were the subject of the will and the donation. Therefore, said Gaudentius, Placida's name ought to appear in the *supplicatio*, but it did not. At this point Symmachus gave up.

GLOSSARY OF LATIN WORDS OCCURRING IN THE TRANSLATION

adiutor. An official in the *officium urbanum*; see *primiscrinius*.

agens in rebus. An imperial agent, appointed by the *magister officiorum*. Originally dispatch-riders or special emissaries, they obtained a bad reputation as spies; their status rose and the senior members of the *schola agentium in rebus* became *principes*, heads of government departments, of which the *officium urbanum* was one. Whether sent on some special enquiry or serving as *principes*, they reported independently to the *magister officiorum*. A department was therefore under constant supervision.

apparitio. The lower staff of the *officium urbanum*.

apparitor. A member of the preceding.

arca quaestoria. A treasury controlled by the senate, also called *arca publica*.

arca vinaria. The treasury responsible for the supply of wine and meat; normally it paid for all public works in Rome except the aqueducts; with these commitments it had some control over certain of the guilds (*corpora*), e.g. masons, lime-burners. It was nominally under the *comes sacrarum largitionum*, but, since local administration was necessary, the prefect of the city was also concerned.

candidatus. A member of a corps of white-uniformed bodyguards of the Emperor. Cf. Amm. 15. 5. 16, 25. 3. 6, 31. 13. 16, 31. 15. 8; Dess. 1174, 2350.

censuales. A department of the *officium urbanum* working in the *secretarium senatus* close to the senate-house and controlled by a *magister censualium*. It kept the list of the senators and their property, and the assessments for taxes and other *munera*; it organized games for absentee senators when it was their duty to give them.

clarissimus. A title given to members of the senate and to provincial governors if they were *consulares*.

cognitionalis. A clerk of the court.

comes. During the principate a member of the Emperor's retinue when he travelled; under Constantine the title of a high official with an assigned sphere of duty. The senior *comites* formed the *comitatus*, court or central government. The title was also conferred as an honour. A *comes* was *illustris*.

GLOSSARY

comes rei privatae. The chief of an imperial department which annexed lapsed properties and administered all lands so acquired, cf. *rationalis*.

comes sacrarum largitionum. The chief financial officer of the Empire, with a large staff in the provinces (for titles and ranks see *CJust*. 12. 23. 7 (384). He received taxes paid in gold and silver (as opposed to in kind) as e.g. the *aurum oblaticium* and *coronarium*; he paid out cash to the army and civil service and also clothing issued as part of pay.

cornicularius. The senior man in the establishment of an imperial department, though above him was the *princeps* appointed by the Emperor. See further p. 8. For the word see Liv. 10. 44. 5, Suet. *gram.* 9, Pseudo-Ascon. 1. 71, Cassiod. 11. 36.

corniculus. Apparently the same as *cornicularius*.

curator. A guardian or agent representing a minor, woman, absentee, etc.

illustris. A higher grade of *clarissimus*; the title was given to *comites*, urban and praetorian prefects, and the *magister officiorum*.

magister officiorum. One of the chief officers of state, ranking as an *illustris*. He was in control of the corps of *agentes in rebus* and of several departments of the central government. He received reports from provincial governors, prefects, army-commanders, judges, and it largely rested with him what documents and persons reached imperial notice; otherwise his department drafted replies on their own initiative.

munerationes. A department dealing with exemptions and privileges.

navicularii. A guild or guilds of shippers, often rich men, who undertook the transport of goods required by the state anywhere in the Empire. Members were granted many immunities. The guilds furnished virtually a merchant navy service for the state.

negotiatores. A guild of members who were required to give their services to the buying, selling, and purveying of the goods furnished at state expense to the cities and particularly Rome. They were given exemption from other state services and received allowances in kind.

nomenclator. An official of the *officium urbanum* who summoned parties to court, and attended on the prefect and acted as bodyguard. Probably the same as *praeco*.

notarius. A secretary to the central offices of government; at first an inferior post, it rose to great importance and in 381 it carried

GLOSSARY

senatorial rank: *CTh.* 6. 10. 2, 3, cf. **23**. **6, 26**. The chief notary could become praetorian prefect or proconsul. He was entrusted with secret missions, personal, diplomatic, military, etc.

perfectissimus. A title given especially to *praesides* of provinces, *principes, cornicularii*, and others.

praeco. Probably the same as *nomenclator*.

praefectus annonae. The prefect in charge of the corn-supply.

primiscrinius. A shortened form of *primiscrinius adiutor* and of *primiscrinius numerarius*, both of the rank of *adiutor*, but senior in position. One was concerned with police matters, the other with finance; their immediate superior was the *cornicularius*.

princeps officii. The chief official in the *officium urbanum*; he was an *agens in rebus* appointed by the *magister officiorum*; he was thus imposed on the department as an agent in the interest of the Emperor. His duties were chiefly judicial, but his control was general; he could give orders to the *tribunus fori suarii* and his soldiers, and he could arrest, **23**. 11, 12. He held the rank of *perfectissimus*, and on retirement could obtain *allectio* (appointment by the Emperor) *inter consulares* and the rank of *clarissimus*.

procurator. An agent.

protector. A member of a special imperial guard organized as a *schola* and admitting centurions of merit, who were then trained and sent to equestrian posts in the Empire, cf. Amm. 14. 7. 9, Dess. 2783, 2785, 2788, 9204. In **41**. 1, 6. = 'guardian'.

rationalis. In full *rationalis rei privatae*. For his duties, see *comes rei privatae*. He had his own staff, and exercised judicial powers in a court of his own.

sacrum aerarium. A general term for imperial funds.

spectabilis. A title given to proconsuls, *vicarii*, and *duces* of the armies.

strator. Originally a groom or equerry in the army. A member of the military staff of *legati*. An official in the offices of the praetorian prefect and of provincial governors such as *correctores*.

suarius. A member of the guild of men connected with the purveying of free pork to the people of Rome.

tribunus et notarius. An official ranking between a *notarius* and the senior posts *primicerius, secundicerius*, and *tertiocerius*. He ranked as *clarissimus*.

tribunus fori suarii. The officer commanding the *contubernales*, who

GLOSSARY

occupied the *castra urbana* in the *Campus Martius* close to the pig-market, and took the place of the urban cohorts.

vicarius. When Diocletian organized the Empire into dioceses, he placed over each a *vicarius* who was a deputy of the praetorian prefect (*vices agens praefecti praetorio*). He had oversight of the administration as a whole, and heard appeals from the provincial governors in his diocese.

SELECT INDEX

acclamatio, p. 1, 9, 10
Acholius, 39
actor, 19. 3, 21. 6, 28. 2, 7
adiutor, 23. 7, Glossary
Africanus, 49
agens in rebus, 23. 8, 24. 2, 31. 2, 38. 4, 49. 2, Glossary
Aggarea, 41
Ammianus, 36. 2
Anniana, 32. 1
annona, annonarius, 18. 2, 23. 2
annonae praefectus, 35. 2
Aphrodisius, 26. 3
apparitio, 34. 7, Glossary
apparitor, 23. 12, 14, 28. 4, 29, 31. 2, Glossary
arca quaestoria, 20. 2, Glossary
arca vinaria, 29. 1, 34. 1, Glossary
archiatrus, 27. 2
Aricia, 49. 3
Arsacidae, 9. 3
aurum oblaticium, 30. 1, 3
Auxentius, 25, 26
Aventius, *see* Sallustius
Avitus, 30. 1

baiulus, 3. 15, 14. 3
basilica atque pons, 25. 2
Basilius, 34. 6 n.
Bassianus, 41. 2
Bassus, Anicius Auchenius, 20. 1 n., 23. 4 f., 34. 7
Batrachia, 38
Bizias, 41. 7
Bonifatius, 23. 8
brevia, 35. 2 n.

Camillus, 4. 3
Campanus, 49. 2
candidatus, 23. 3, Glossary
Capua, 40. 4
Carneades, 5. 2
carruca, 4, 20. 1, 23. 8
Castor, 30. 1

castrensis, 14. 4, 42, cf. *militia*
Cattianilla, 30
Catulus, 48
Celsus, 5. 2
Celsus, Ragonius Vincentius, 23. 3 n.
censuales, 23. 2, Glossary
Cerealis, Naeratius, 40. 4 n.
Christiana lex, 21. 1, 6
clarissimus, Glossary
Clitomachus, 5. 2
coerceo, 26. 6
cognitionalis, 4. 7, Glossary
cohortes urbanae, 42
collectarii, 29. 1
comes, 20. 3, 23. 1, 25. 1, Glossary
comes rei privatae, 41. 6, Glossary
comes sacrarum largitionum, 20. 3, Glossary
comitatus sacer, 26. 3
condita, 20. 2
Constans, 40. 2
Constantine, 39. 3, 5, 40. 2
Constantius, 3. 4, 6, 33, 34. 2, 5, 40. 2
constitutio, 33. 4
cornicularius, 33. 3, Glossary
corniculus, 42, Glossary
corpora, 'property', 19. 9
corpora, corporatus, 'guilds', 14, 29. 1, 33, 44. 2
curator, 19. 1, 7, 39. 2, Glossary
curiales, 28. 5
Cyriades, 25, 26

Damasus, 21. 3 n.
decennalia, 13. 2
decuriones, 38. 5
denuntiare litem, 32. 1, 3
disceptator, 39. 5
discepto, 38. 2
discussio, discussor, 26. 2, 34. 3, 6, 9
Donatus, 48. 3

Epictetus, 27. 2
Euphasius, 16. 1

244

INDEX

Eupraxius, Flavius, **32.** 1 n.
Eusebius, **48.** 1
excipere quaestionem, **32.** 2
executor, **48.** 2

Fariana, **28.** 7
Felix, **23.** 7
fiscus, **3.** 12, 13, **41.** 1, 7, **48.** 4
Flavianus, **32.** 1
forma, **20.** 2
Fulgentius, **23.** 6

Gaudentius, *curator*, **19.** 1
Gaudentius, *agens in rebus*, **23.** 8
gleba, **46.** 1
Gratianus, **34.** 9, 11, **40.** 4

Hannibal, **3.** 9
Heliodorus, **41.** 7
Hesperius, **23.** 1 n.
Hyginus, **49.** 2

illustris, Glossary
immodicae donationes, **19.** 7
indicta, **28.** 5
invasio, **28.** 1
Iohannes, **27.** 2
Iunior, **31.** 2

Julian, **19.** 4, **34.** 6, **40.** 3

Liberius, **19.** 1
Lolliana, **30.** 1
Lupus, Virius (?), **40.** 3 n.

Macedonius, **36.** 2 n., **44.** 1, 3
magister officiorum, **22.** 3, **34.** 8, **43.** 2, **44.** 1, Glossary
Mamertinus, Claudius, **40.** 4 n.
mancipes salinarum, **44.** 1
mando, **19.** 2, 3, **28.** 7
Marcellus, **38**
Marciana, **19**
Marcianus, **41**
massa, **28.** 2
Maximus, Valerius, **34.** 5 n.
mechanicus, **26.** 1
medici, **27**
Memorius, **23.** 4

militia, **27.** 2, **38.** 5, **42, 49.** 4
milito, **23.** 8, **48.** 3
moderator, **38.** 2, **40.** 1
momenti reformatio, **28.** 1, 10
munerationes, **30.** 1, Glossary
Murcia vallis, **9.** 6
Musa, **39**

navicularii, **44.** 2, 3, Glossary
negotiatores, **14.** 1, Glossary
Nigrinianus, **34.** 3
nomenclator, **23.** 8, Glossary
notarius, **18.** 2, **23.** 6, **26,** Glossary
notoria, **25.** 3
novatio, **32.** 3
nummularius, **29.** 1

oblatio, **13.** 2
oblativae functiones, **30.** 1
officium urbanum, p.
oleum, **14.** 3, **35.** 2
Olybrius, Quintus Clodius Hermogenianus, **28** n.
Orfitus, **34.** 8 n., 10

palatia (pl.), **9.** 2
palatina castra, **38.** 5
palatina militia, **27.** 2
palatinus, **23.** 8, **48.** 1
palatinus munerationum sacrarum, **30.** 1
palatium, **27.** 4
patrocinium, **28.** 5
perfectissimus, Glossary
Petronianus, **42**
Placida, **19.** 7
Polemonianus, **16.** 1
Pompey, theatre of, **6.** 2, **9.** 3
praeco, **23.** 5, 8, Glossary
praefectura praetoriana, **35.** 2
praefectura urbana, **48.** 1
praefectus annonae, **23.** 2, **35.** 2, Glossary
praescriptio, **19.** 2, 3
Praetextatus, Vettius Agorius, **10** n., **11, 12, 21.** 5, 24
primiscrinius, **34.** 6, Glossary
princeps officii, **23.** 10, Glossary
Principius, **19.** 2
Prisca, **19.** 6

INDEX

Priscianus, 16. 1
pro indiviso, 28. 7
procurator, 19. 1, 28. 6, 32. 1, Glossary
protector, 32. 1, 36. 2, 41. 1, 6, Glossary
Publicola, 4. 3
Puteoli, 40

rationalis, 41. 1, 2, 5, 6, Glossary
rector, 1. 3, 34. 11, 40. 3
reformo, 33. 2
reparatio, 19. 3, 4, 32. 2, 38. 4, 39. 3
res privata, see *comes*
restauratio integri, 39. 2
Roma, 3. 9
Rusticiana, 34. 12 n.

sacrum aerarium, 13. 3, Glossary
sacrum auditorium, 40. 1, 5, 41. 6
Sallustius Aventius, 23. 4 n., 34. 7
Salmoneus, 4. 2
Sarmatae, 47. 1
Scirtius, 28. 2
scrinia, 24. 1, p. 8
scrinia palatina, 21. 6
secretarium circi, 23. 9
secretarium commune, 23. 4, cf. 23. 8
secretarium Tellurense, p. 8
securitas, 29. 2, 4
sedes praetoriana, 31. 2
sedes quae vicem principum tuetur, 41. 6
sedes sacra, 39. 4
sedes urbana, 23. 6
sedes vicaria, 23. 3
Sergius, 34. 3 n.
Severilla, 30. 1
solidi, 29
species, 35. 2, 3

spectabilis, Glossary
strator, 38. 2, Glossary
strenae, 15
suarius, 33. 2, Glossary
supplementum (in legal sense), 19. 7
Symmachus, L. Aurelius Avianus . . . Phosphorius, p. 9
Symmachus, Q. Aurelius . . . Eusebius, pp. 9-14.
Syntrophius, 39. 2

Tarpeius, 28. 6
Tarquinius, 4. 3
Tarracina, 40
Tatius, 15. 1
Terentius, 34 introd. n.
Tertullus, 34. 5 n.
Theodorus, 32. 1
Theodosius, father of the Emperor, 9. 4 n., 43. 2
Theodosius (not the Emperor), 33. 2
thesaurus, 20. 2
Theseus, 28
tribunus et notarius, 23. 6, 26. 3, Glossary
tribunus fori suarii, 22, Glossary
tuitio, 23. 8

Valerianus, 31 n.
vehiculum publicum, 24. 3
Venantius, 38
Vestales virgines, 3. 7, 11, 15
vicaria potestas, 23. 11, 14, 38. 2
vicarius, 23. 3, 26. 3, 33. 2, Glossary
Victor, 23. 8
Victoria, 3. 3
Viventius, 30. 3 n.

LIBRARY OF DAVIDSON COLLEGE

Books on regular loan may be checked out for **two weeks.** Books must be presented at the Circulation Desk in order to be renewed.

A fine is charged after date due.

Special books are subject to special regulations at the discretion of library staff.

OCT 15 1975 APR. -5, 1977 APR. 16, 1977			